Dean Ippolito, LLC

Chess Tactics for Scholastic Players

Table of Contents

How to Use This Workbook	3
How Much Do You Know About Chess?	4
Chess Notation	7
Chapter 1- Checkmate in 1	9
Mate in 3 Ways	10
Mate in 1-Rooks	13
Mate in 1-Queens	19
Mate in 1-Bishops	24
Mate in 1-Knights	28
Mate in 1-Pawns	32
Mate in 1	34
Chapter 2-Chess Tactics	38
Double Attack	39
Double Attacks-Pawns	42
Double Attacks-Knights	44
Double Attacks-Bishops	46
Double Attacks-Rooks	48
Double Attacks-Queens	50
Double Attacks-Kings	52
Double Attacks-1 move	53
Double Attacks-2 moves	55
Double Attacks-3 moves or more!	61
Remove the Guard & Deflection	65
Remove the Guard & Deflection-Difficult!	71
Pin	72
Pins-1 move	75
Pins-2 moves	77
Pins-2 moves-Difficult!	78
Skewer	79
Skewers-1 move	81
Skewers-2 moves	82
Chapter 3-Checkmate in 2 moves	83
Mate in 2-Remove the Guard & Deflection	95
Mate in 2-Square Clearance	100
Mate in 2-Queen and Helper	102
Mate in 2-Difficult!	104
Mate in 2-Very Difficult!	107

Table of Contents

Chapter 4-Checkmate in 3 Moves   109

    Mate in 3-First Move Is Not Check   115

    Mate in 3-Back Rank   117

    Mate in 3-Smothered Mate   120

    Mate in 3-Queen and Helper   122

    Mate in 3-Using A Pin   123

    Mate in 3-Using A Double Check   124

    Mate in 3-Using the h-file   126

    Mate in 3-Difficult!   129

Chapter 5-Mate in 4 Moves   135

Chapter 6-Legall's Checkmates   138

    Legall's Checkmate Problems-Mate in 1   141

    Legall's Checkmate Problems-Mate in 2   142

    Legall's Checkmate Problems-Difficult!   143

Chapter 7- Triple Loyd's   144

Chapter 8- Frame by Frames   147

    Frame by Frame-Smothered Mate   148

    Frame by Frame-King Run   149

    Frame by Frame-h-file   150

    Frame by Frame-Back Rank   152

    Frame by Frame-Queen and Helper   154

    Frame by Frame-Remove the Guard   156

    Frame by Frame-Morphy's Mates   157

Chapter 9-Endgames- From Easy to Hard   158

    2 Rooks and King vs. King   161

    Queen and King vs. King   168

    Rook and King vs. King   174

    King and Pawn Endgames   180

    King and Pawn Endings-Some Key Positions   181

    King and Pawn Endings-Test   182

How Much Do You Know About Chess Answers   192

Answers to Exercises   193

How the Pieces Move Reference Page   203

Glossary   204

How to Use This Workbook

As a student and teacher of chess, I have often been frustrated by the lack of material available for the beginning to intermediate scholastic player. There are many tactics workbooks available, but most do not present the material in a way which slowly reinforces the same patterns until that pattern has been mastered by the student. This can cause particular problems for the younger students. This workbook is designed to fill in those gaps. I have also found that it is a useful teaching aid in the classroom and will challenge but not frustrate the majority of scholastic players. Many examples are taken from practical games using themes that are likely to occur. Many problems are also taken directly from some of the most instructive positions of my students. You will even find a few positions that have been taken directly from my own games.

While some parts of this workbook will be challenging for tournament players with ratings as high as 1800, it is geared more for players up to a strength of 1400. This workbook is unique in that I have made every effort to make the pattern recognition parts of this workbook as beneficial as possible in the following way: these problems do not just reinforce themes but the same patterns within those themes. This is the most effective way to have even the youngest students recognize patterns quickly.

There are several parts to this workbook ranging from tactics to endgames. The student is encouraged to start at the beginning of the workbook and work through. However, if some students feel the beginning sections are too easy they may want to skip ahead. In order to give you a better idea of where to begin, there is a 3 page test at the beginning. Based on your score, you can then determine where to start. The point values are listed next to each question and you will need to add the total points to receive your score. For the tournament player, the test should not take more than a few minutes.

Most critical areas of a chess game are covered and can be improved in this workbook. Included are chess tactics problems, checkmate problems, pattern recognition problems, classic checkmate ideas, and key endgame positions. If you see a word that is unfamiliar to you, please refer to the glossary at the back of the workbook, or use a regular dictionary.

Good luck!

Dean Ippolito
International Master of Chess

How Much Do You Know About Chess?
Circle your answer from the choices below:

1. Which chess piece cannot move backward?

A) pawn   B) knight   C) king   D) bishop

1 point

2. Which is the only chess piece that can jump over other pieces?

A) pawn   B) knight   C) queen   D) king

1 point

3. Which is the only chess piece that can NEVER be captured?

A) rook   B) knight   C) queen   D) king

1 point

4. Which chess piece is the most powerful?

A) pawn   B) rook   C) queen   D) king

1 point

5. Can you ever move two chess pieces at the same time?

A) Yes   B) No

2 points

6. What happens when a pawn gets to the other end of the board?

A) it does a little dance   B) it turns into a queen   C) it can turn into any piece
D) it can turn into a queen, rook, knight, or bishop only

2 points

7. What is it called if a king is under attack, but can get out of it?

A) check   B) checkmate   C) stalemate   D) leave my king alone

2 points

8. What is it called if a king is under attack, but cannot get out it?

A) check   B) checkmate   C) stalemate   D) leave my king alone

2 points

9. What is it called if a king is not under attack and he has no legal moves for any of his pieces?

A) check   B) checkmate   C) stalemate   D) leave my king alone

2 points

10-12. List the three ways to get a king out of attack:

__block__   __go away__   _____

1 point each

13. How many points is a pawn worth?

A) 1   B) 2   C) 5   D) 0

1 point

14. How many points is a queen worth?

A) 5   B) 7   C) 9   D) 10   1 point

15-16. In the diagram, circle the two pieces that the Black knight can capture?

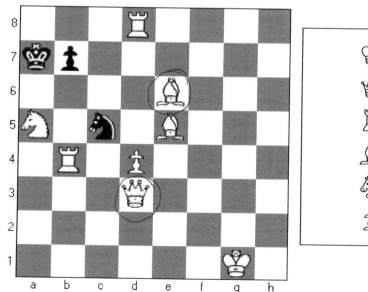

KEY

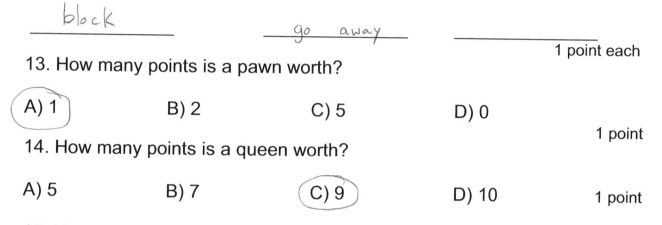

♔ — King
♕ — Queen
♖ — Rook
♗ — Bishop
♘ — Knight
♙ — Pawn

1 point each

17. In the diagram, circle the White piece that is attacking the Black king:

18. In the diagram, draw an arrow to show how the Black king can get out of attack:

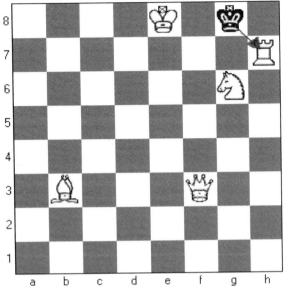

1 point each

19-20. Draw an arrow to show how White can checkmate Black in one move in each diagram:

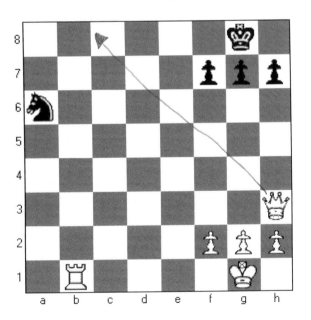 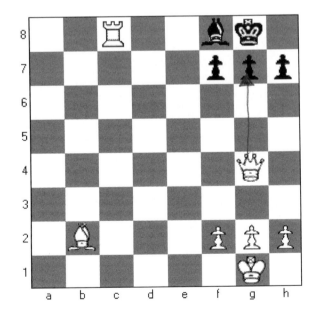

2 points each

Answers on page 192

Chess Notation

Chess notation will make it easier to understand and read the language of chess. It is fairly simple to use once you know the trick. Your parents will be very impressed that you are able to learn and speak chess language!

Chess notation tells us where pieces move. If we want to say a king moved to a certain square we would have to name that square. Each of the 64 squares has a name.

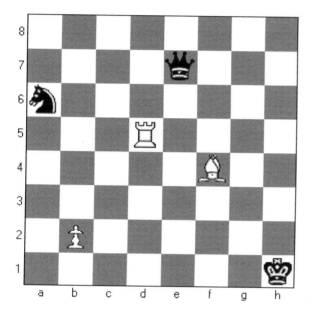

On the board above, Black's king is on the square h1.

Here are more examples of naming squares:

The pawn is on b2.
The bishop is on f4.
The rook is on d5.
The knight is on a6.
The queen is on e7.

All we did was to name the squares. That is the hardest part. Let's now talk about how we can use that knowledge to help us learn chess notation.

Chess Notation

When writing chess notation, there are two parts to writing down a move. The first part is naming the piece that is moving. The second part is the name of the square. When naming a square we ALWAYS name the letter before the number.

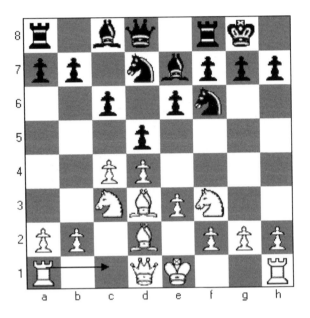

It's White's turn. He wants to move the rook over two as shown. We would write this as follows: Rc1

R stands for rook. C1 means the rook moved to c1. That's all there is to it!

Here are the abbreviations for the other pieces:
B=bishop
Q=queen
K=king
N=knight (even though we know that knight starts with a K and not an N, we save the letter K for king)
P= pawn

This is the easiest way to use chess notation for right now.
Here are the remaining symbols:

Castling kingside= 0-0
Castling queenside= 0-0-0
Check= +
Checkmate= ++
Captures= x

Chapter 1-Checkmate in 1 Move

In this chapter, you will need to find how White can attack Black's king without Black being able to get out of the attack. This is what we call checkmate. The king has no escape by either moving away to a safe square, capturing the piece that is attacking him, or putting a defender between himself and the opponent's attacking piece (blocking). This section, as with the rest of the workbook, will start out easily and gradually get more challenging. In the first problems, you will have to find three different ways to make a checkmate in 1 move. That is a warm-up for the rest of the chapter where you will only need to find one way to make a checkmate in 1 move.

If you are an experienced player, please feel free to use this chapter as a warm-up. If you'd like to challenge yourself, try to complete the entire chapter in under 30 minutes. See how you stack up against an experienced chess master. Most experienced chess masters can finish all of chapter 1 in 5 minutes!

Good luck!

Mate in 3 Ways #1

Draw arrows to show how White can checkmate in 1 move 3 different ways

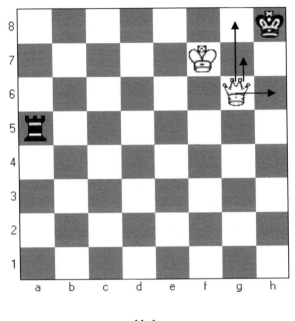

#1

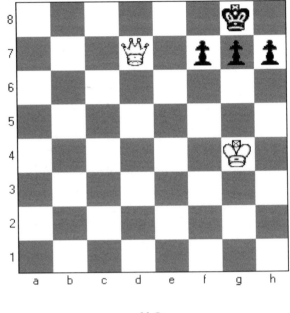

#2

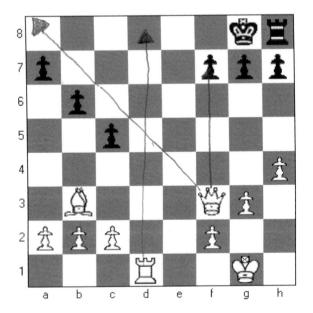

#3

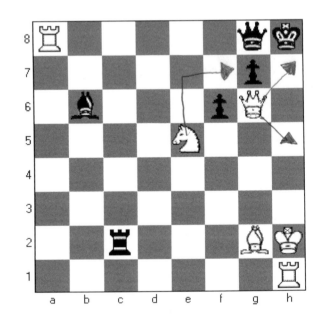

#4

Mate in 3 Ways #2

Draw arrows to show how White can checkmate in 1 move 3 different ways

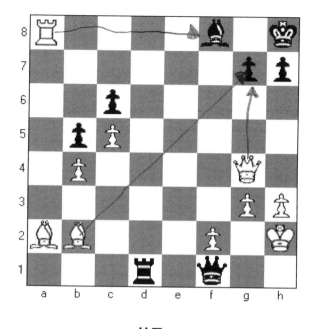

#5

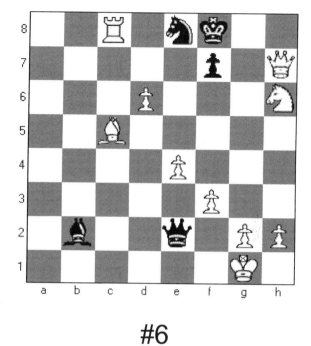

#6

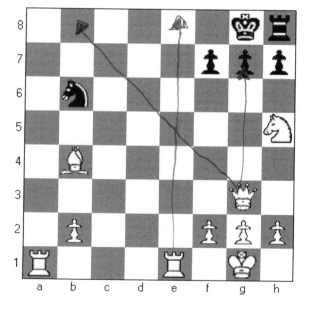

#7

#8

Mate in 3 Ways #3

Draw arrows to show how White can checkmate in 1 move 3 different ways

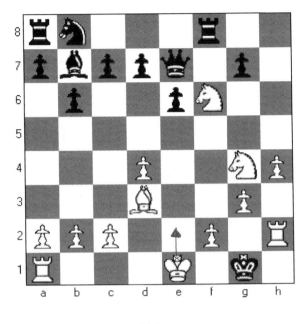

#9

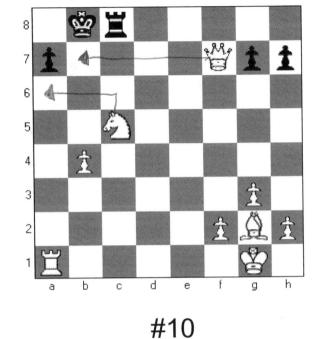

#10

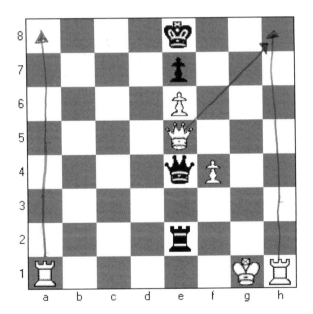

#11

#12

Mate in 1-Rooks

Draw an arrow or use chess notation to show how White can checkmate in one move

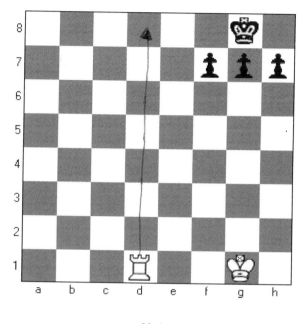

#1

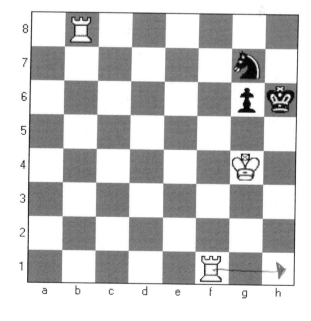

#2

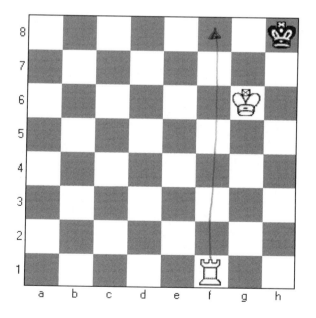

#3

#4

Mate in 1-Rooks

Draw an arrow or use chess notation to show how White can checkmate in one move

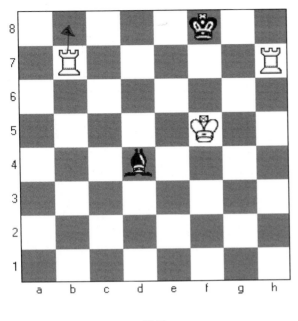

#5

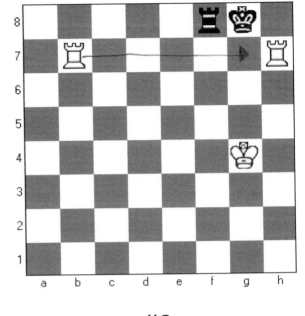

#6

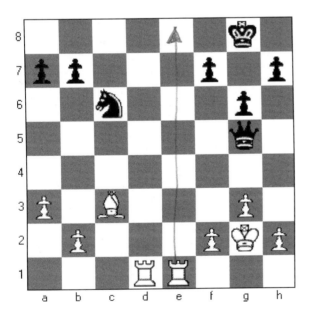

#7

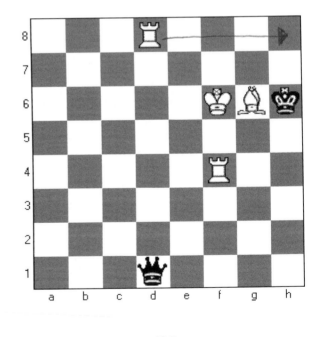

#8

Mate in 1-Rooks

Draw an arrow or use chess notation to show how White can checkmate in one move

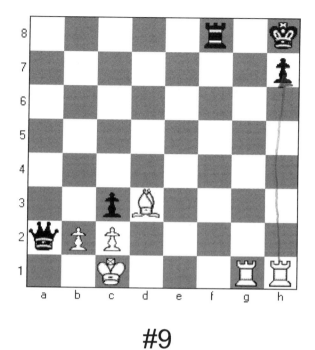

#9

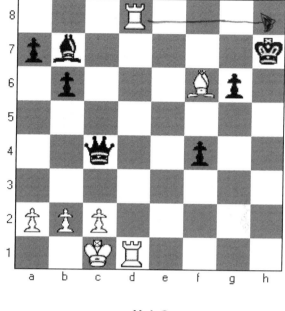

#10

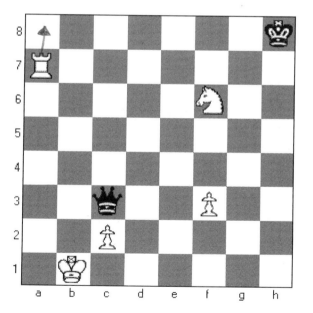

#11

#12

Mate in 1-Rooks

Draw an arrow or use chess notation to show how White can checkmate in one move

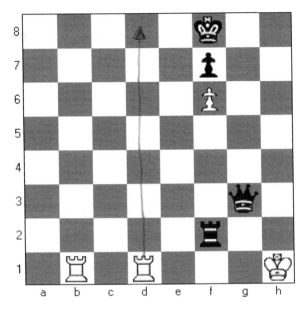

#13

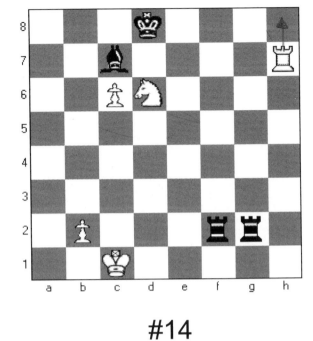

#14

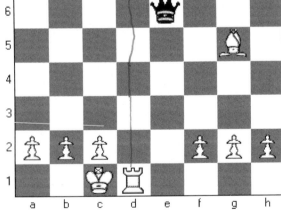

#15

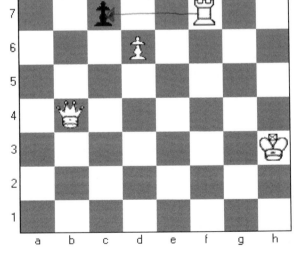

#16

Mate in 1-Rooks

Draw an arrow or use chess notation to show how White can checkmate in one move

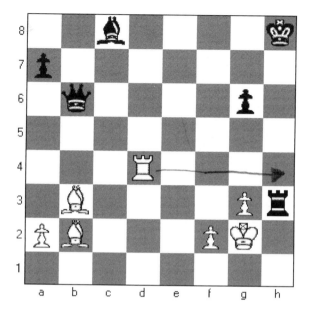

#17

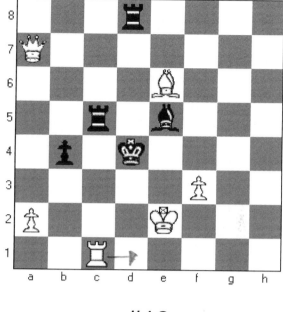

#18

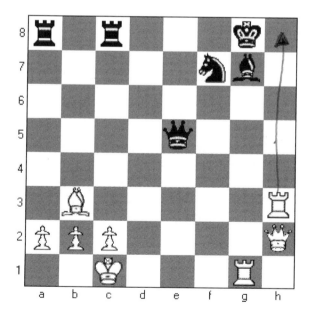

#19

#20

Mate in 1-Rooks

Draw an arrow or use chess notation to show how White can checkmate in one move

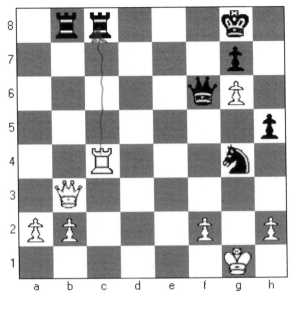

#21

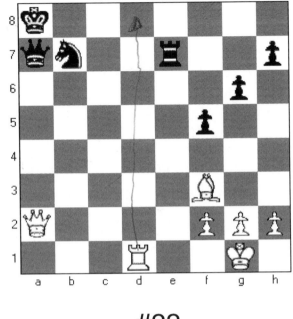

#22

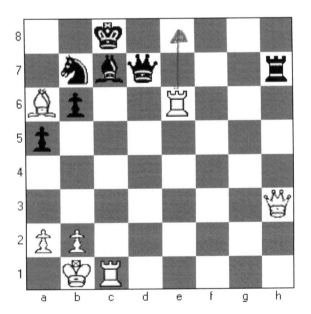

#23

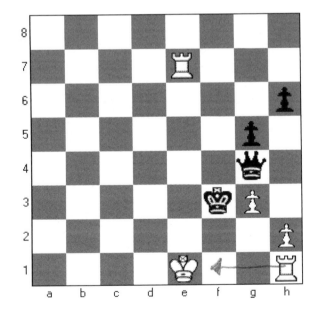

#24

Mate in 1-Queens

Draw an arrow or use chess notation to show how White can checkmate in one move

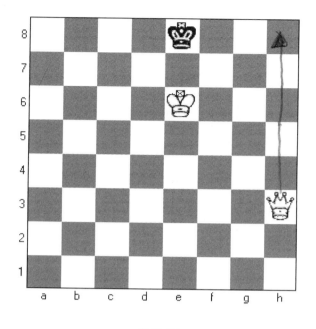

#25

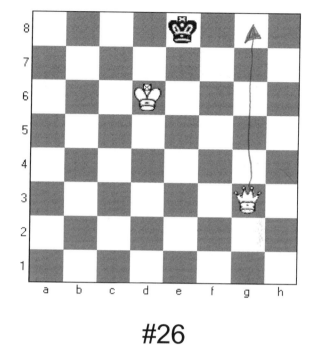

#26

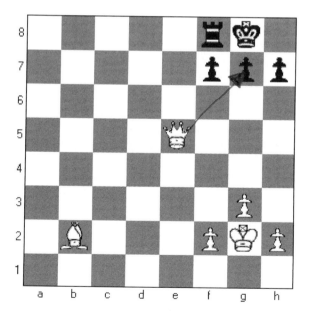

#27

#28

Mate in 1-Queens

Draw an arrow or use chess notation to show how White can checkmate in one move

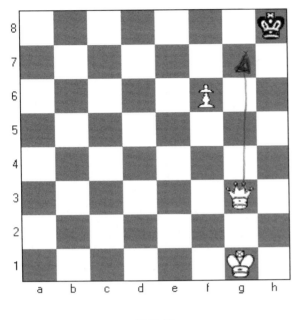

#29

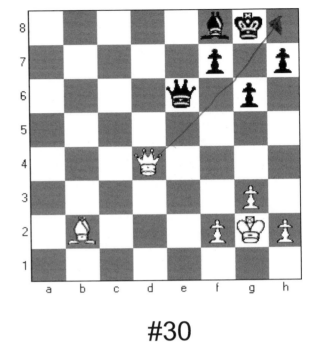

#30

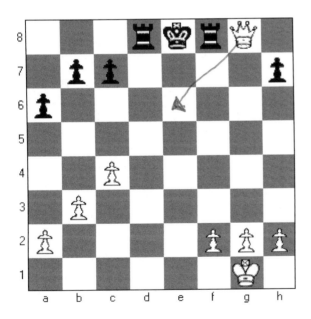

#31

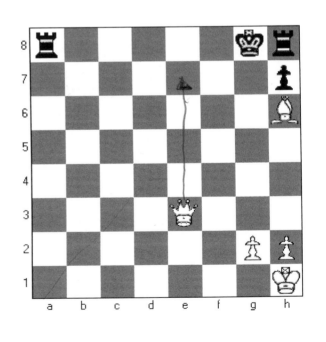

#32

Mate in 1-Queens

Draw an arrow or use chess notation to show how White can checkmate in one move

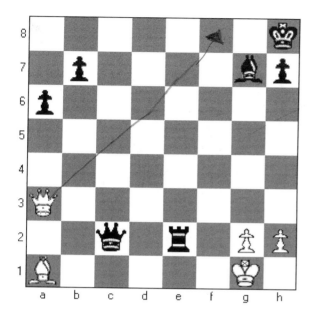

#33

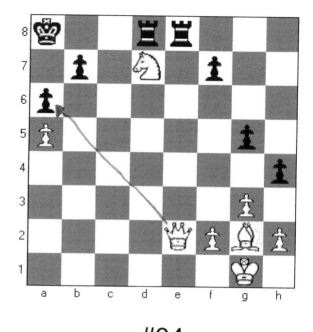

#34

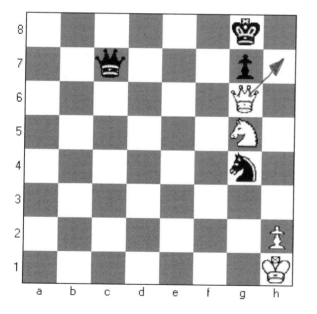

#35

#36

Mate in 1-Queens

Draw an arrow or use chess notation to show how White can checkmate in one move

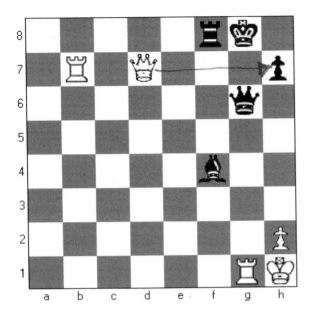

#37

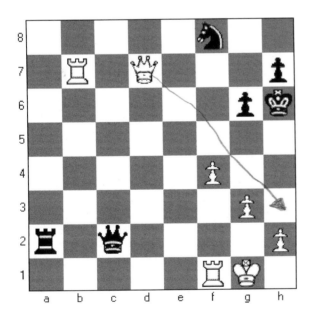

#39

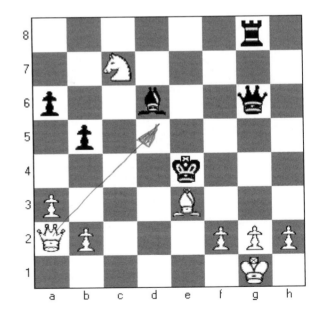

#38

#40

Mate in 1-Queens

Draw an arrow or use chess notation to show how White can checkmate in one move

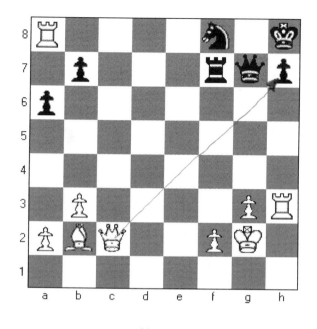

#41

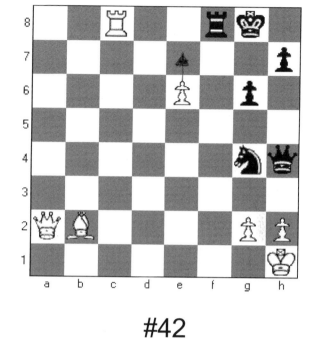

#42

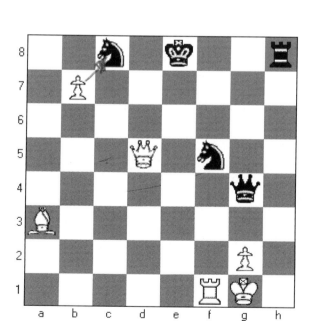

#43

#44

Mate in 1-Bishops

Draw an arrow or use chess notation to show how White can checkmate in one move

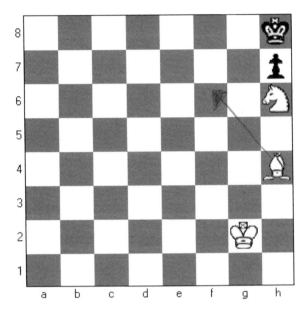

#45

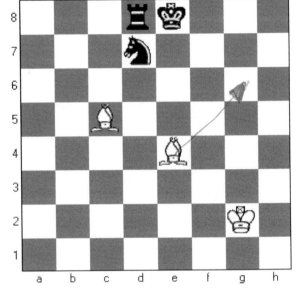

#46

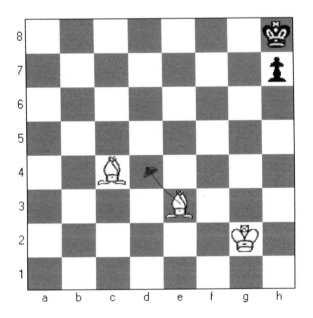

#47

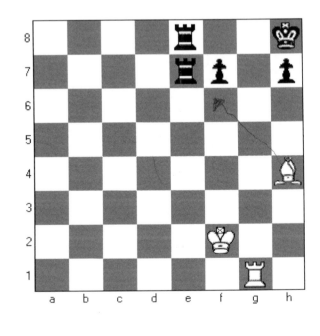

#48

Mate in 1-Bishops

Draw an arrow or use chess notation to show how White can checkmate in one move

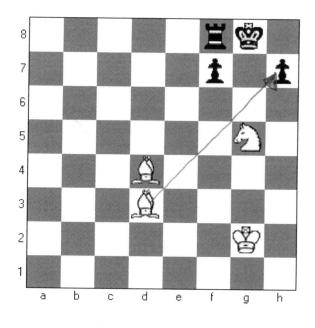

#49

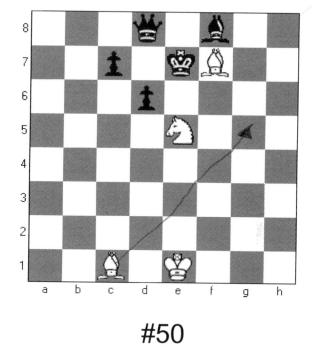

#50

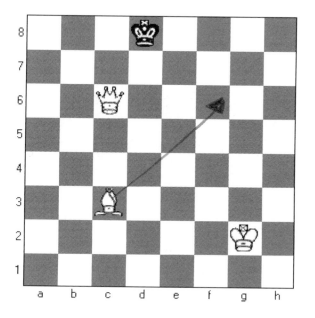

#51

#52

Mate in 1-Bishops

Draw an arrow or use chess notation to show how White can checkmate in one move

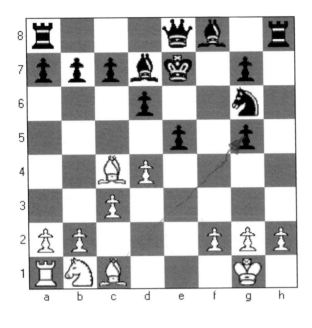

#53

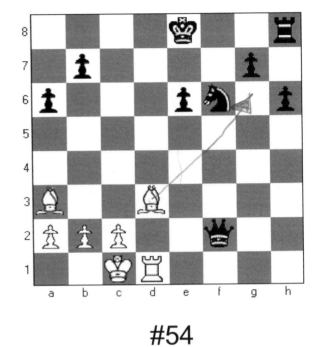

#54

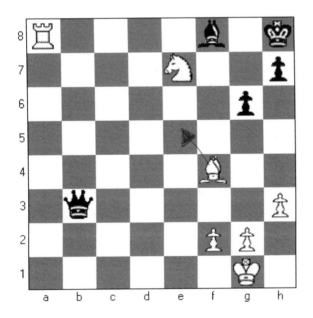

#55

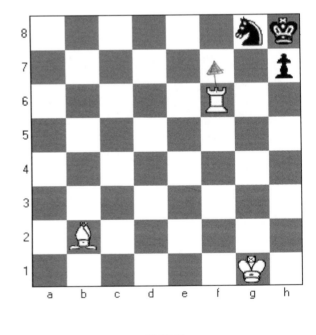

#56

Mate in 1-Bishops

Draw an arrow or use chess notation to show how White can checkmate in one move

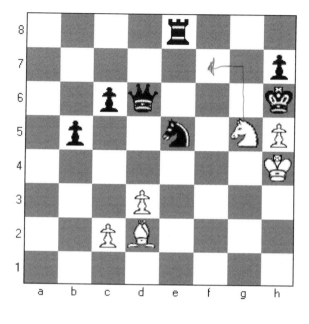

#57

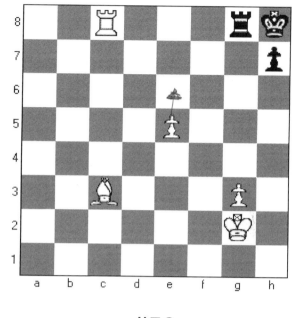

#58

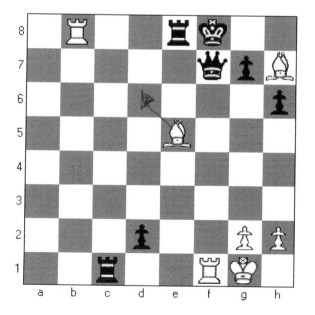

#59

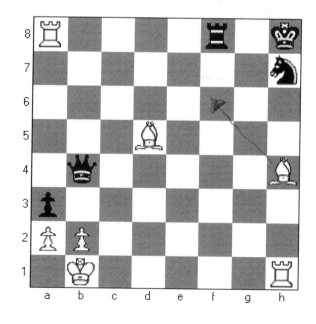

#60

Mate in 1-Knights

Draw an arrow or use chess notation to show how White can checkmate in one move

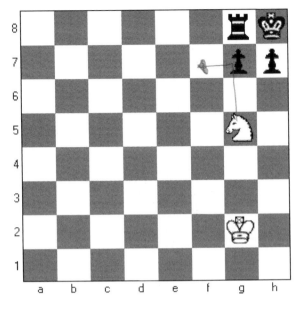

#61

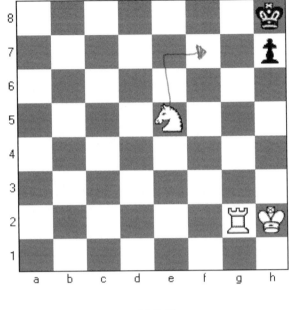

#62

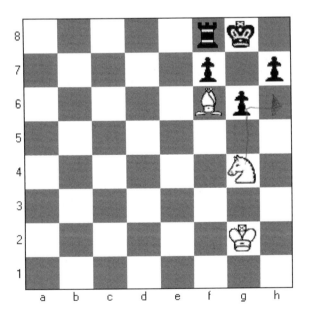

#63

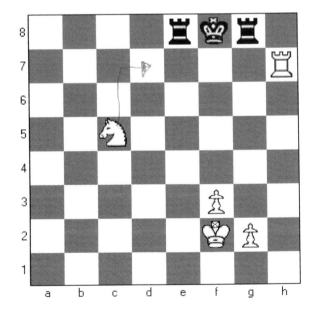

#64

Mate in 1-Knights

Draw an arrow or use chess notation to show how White can checkmate in one move

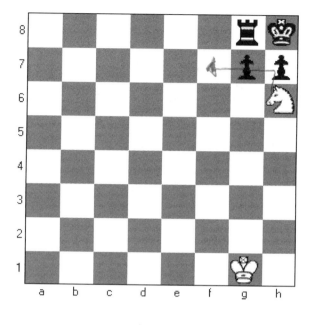

#65

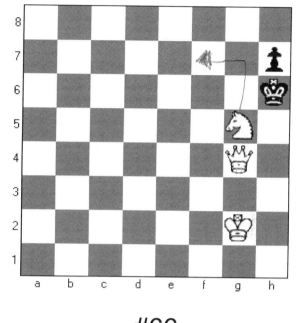

#66

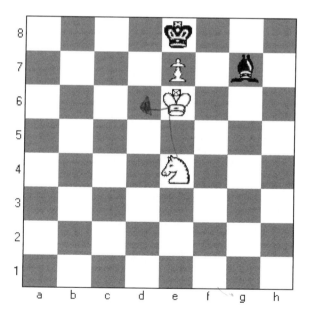

#67

#68

Mate in 1-Knights

Draw an arrow or use chess notation to show how White can checkmate in one move

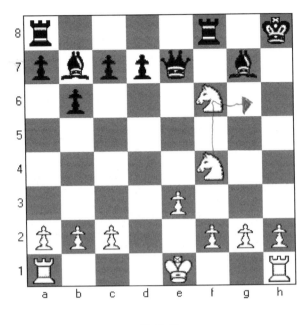

#69

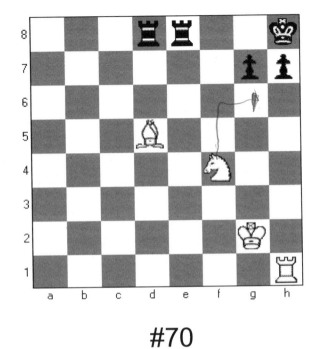

#70

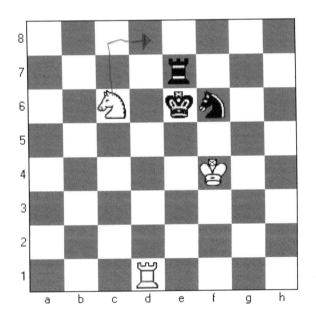

#71

#72

Mate in 1-Knights

Draw an arrow or use chess notation to show how White can checkmate in one move

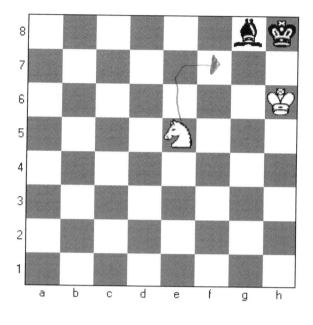

#73

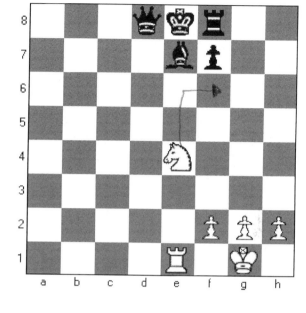

#74

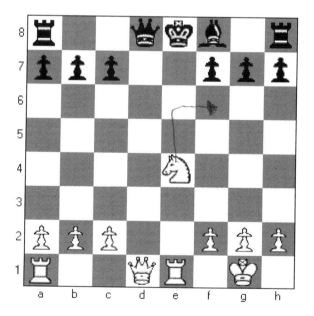

#75

promote to knight

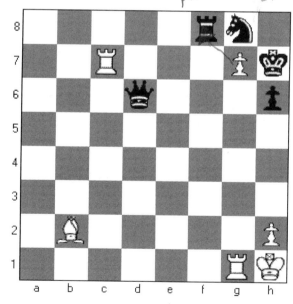

#76

Mate in 1-Pawns

Draw an arrow or use chess notation to show how White can checkmate in one move

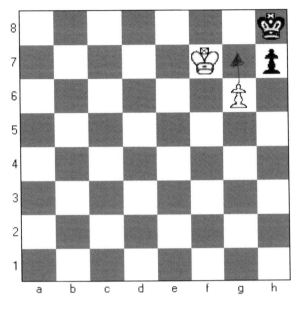

#77

#78

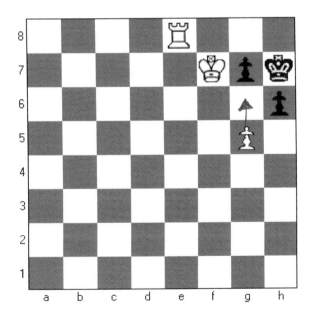

#79

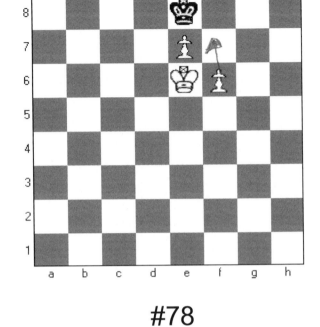

#80

Mate in 1-Pawns

Draw an arrow or use chess notation to show how White can checkmate in one move

#81

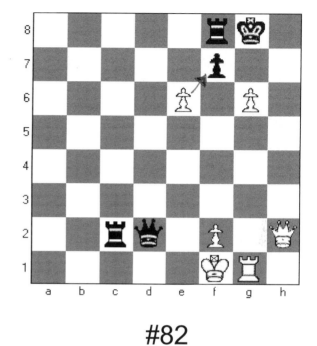

#82

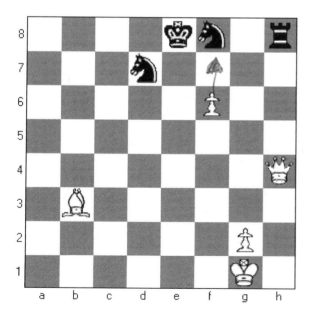

#83

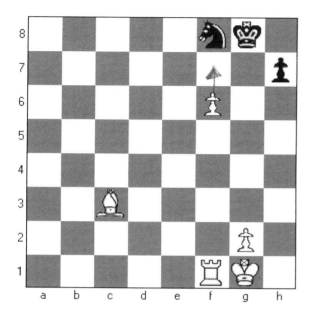

#84

Mate in 1

Draw an arrow or use chess notation to show how White can checkmate in one move

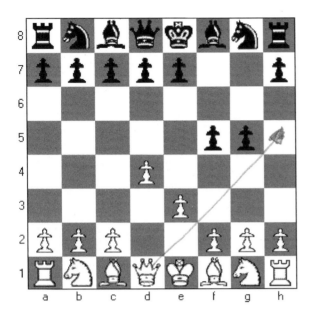

#85

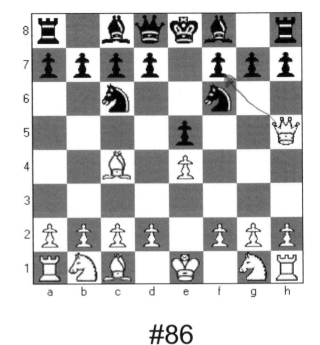

#86

#87

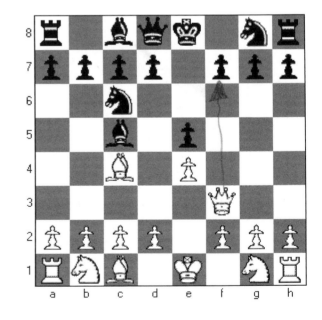

#88

Mate in 1

Draw an arrow or use chess notation to show how White can checkmate in one move

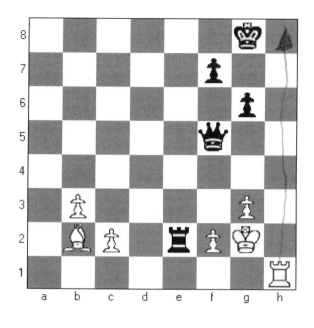

#89

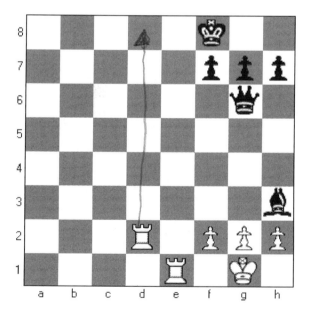

#91

#90

#92

Mate in 1

Draw an arrow or use chess notation to show how White can checkmate in one move

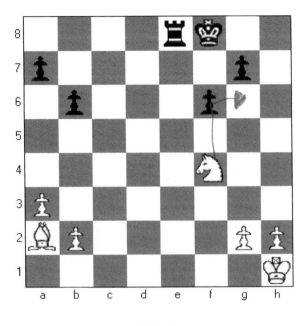

#93

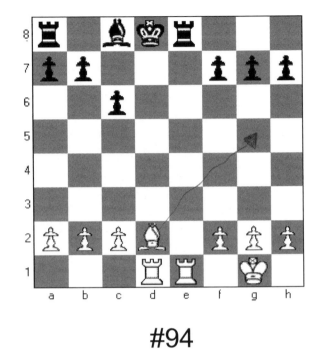

#94

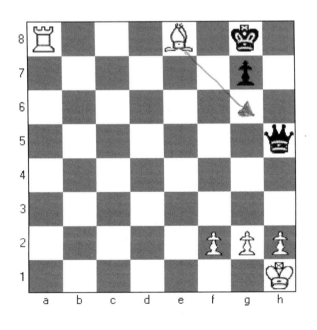

#95

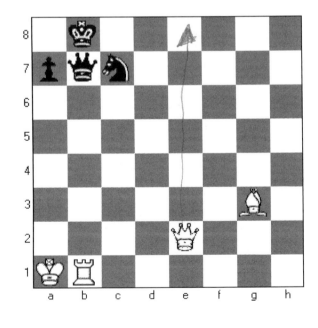

#96

Mate in 1

Draw an arrow or use chess notation to show how White can checkmate in one move

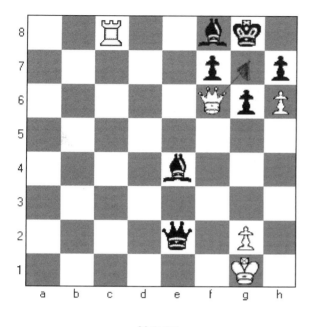

#97

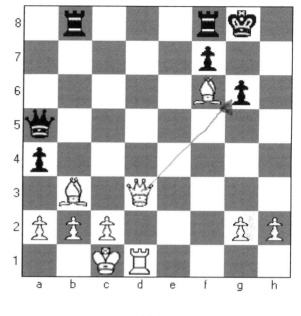

#98

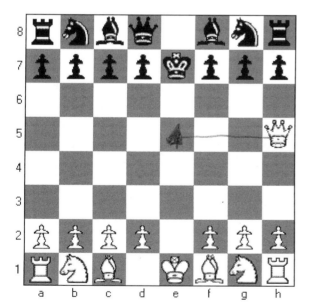

#99

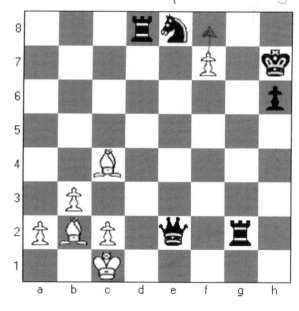

#100

Chapter 2-Chess Tactics

This chapter will introduce many of the basic chess tactics that can be used to help win a chess game. It will start out with an explanation of the chess tactic and then give some simple examples. After you familiarize yourself with the idea, you can then see how well you understand the tactic by going on to the exercises.

Good luck!

Chess Tactics-Double Attack

There are many different tactics that can be used to help win the game. Let's take a look at some of them. First, the **double attack**. A double attack (also known as a **fork**) is when one piece attacks two pieces at the same time, making it impossible for your opponent to save both attacked pieces. A double attack can also be when a piece is attacking one piece and making a big threat (like checkmate). There are **effective** double attacks and **ineffective** double attacks. Let's take a look at the difference.

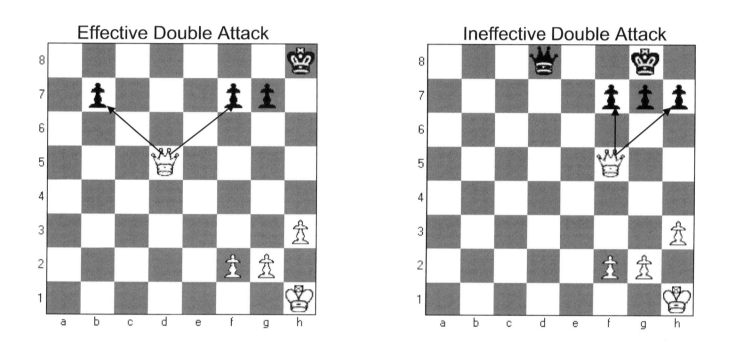

In the first diagram, the White queen attacks both the f7 and b7 pawns. Both pawns are not being defended. Black cannot protect both of them at the same time.

In the second diagram, the White queen attacks both the f7 and h7 pawns. However, both pawns are protected by the Black king. If the White queen were to capture either Black pawn, she would be captured back by the Black king. This would not be a good situation for White since a queen is a more powerful piece than a pawn. I call moves that give up big pieces for less valuable pieces '**Happy Birthdays**'. It's like giving your opponent a nice birthday present!

Chess Tactics

Now let's take a look at some simple double attacks together.

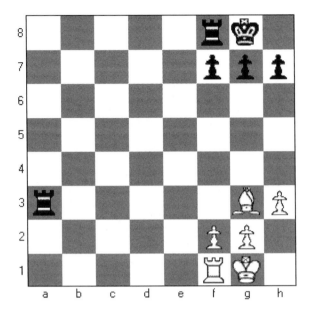

Q: Can the White bishop move to attack both Black rooks at the same time? ✓

A: The White bishop can move to d6 where it threatens to capture both Black rooks.

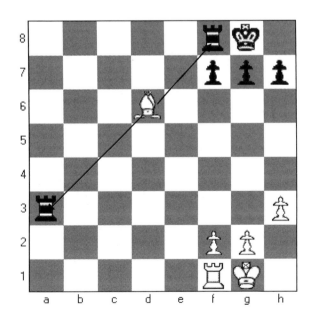

There is no way that Black can save both rooks. One will be captured by the bishop on White's next move.

Chess Tactics

Q: How can White attack two Black pieces at once?

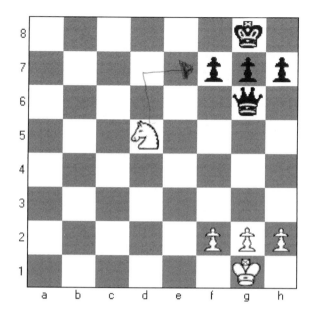

A: The White knight can move to e7 where it attacks both the Black king and the Black queen.

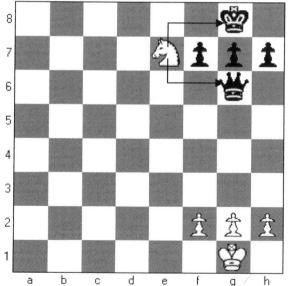

There is no way that Black can save both the king and the queen. Since a king can never be captured, he will have to move. Once the king moves, White's knight will capture Black's queen.

Now you are going to find your own double attacks. We will start with one move double attacks, and then work to more difficult ones.

Double Attacks-Pawns

Draw an arrow to show how White can use a double attack to win material

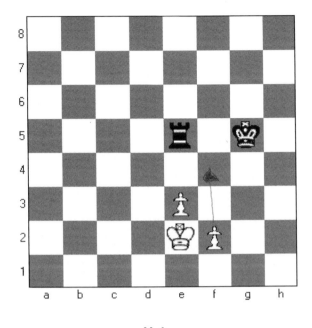

#1

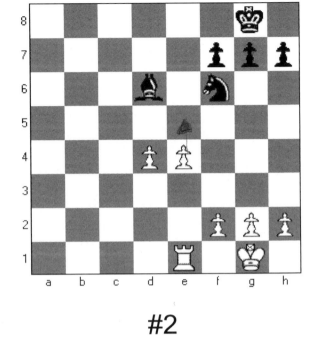

#2

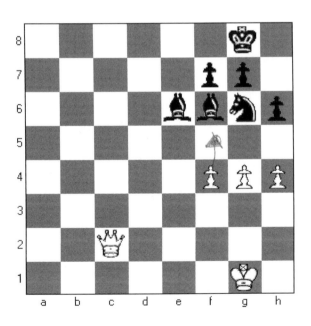

#3

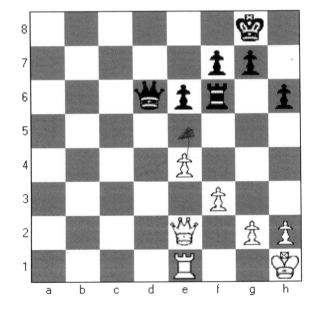

#4

Double Attacks-Pawns

Draw an arrow to show how White can use a double attack to win material

#5

#6

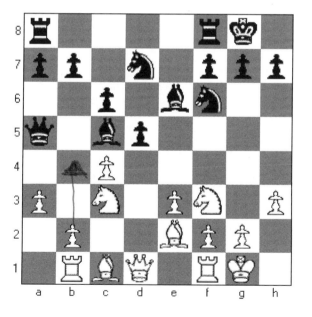

#7

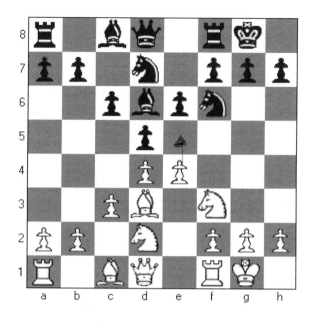

#8

Double Attacks-Knights

Draw an arrow to show how White can use a double attack to win material

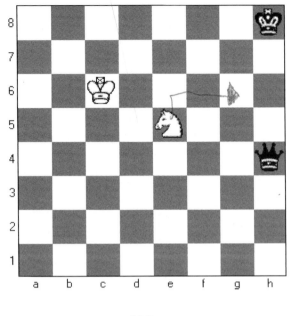

#9

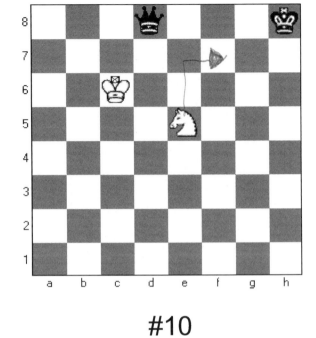

#10

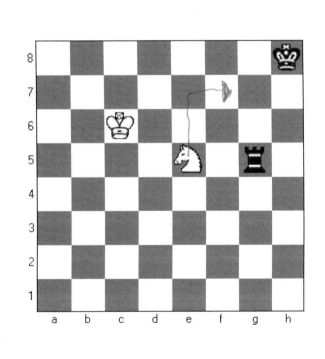

#11

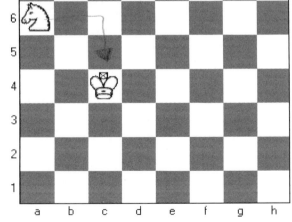

#12

Double Attacks-Knights

Draw an arrow to show how White can use a double attack to win material

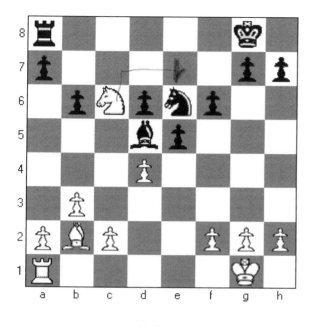

#13

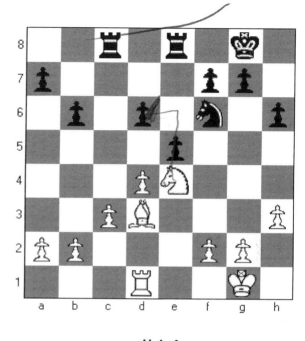

#14

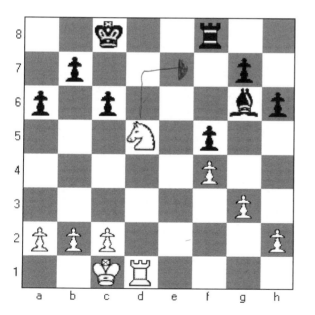

#15

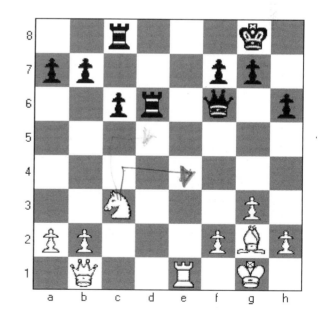

#16

Double Attacks-Bishops

Draw an arrow to show how White can use a double attack to win material

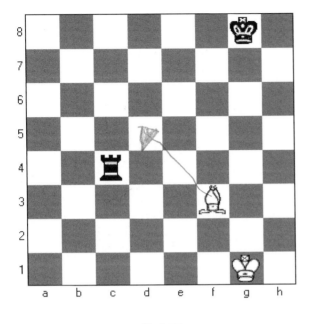

#17

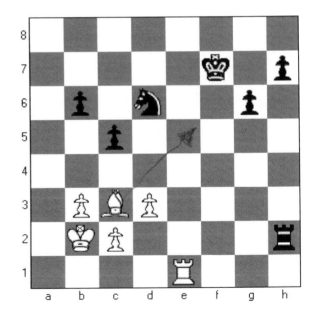

#18

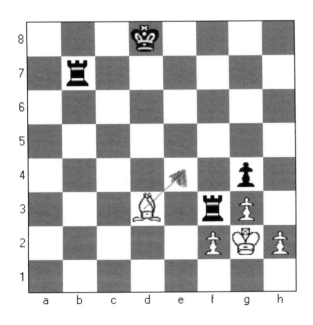

#19

#20

Double Attacks-Bishops

Draw an arrow to show how White can use a double attack to win material

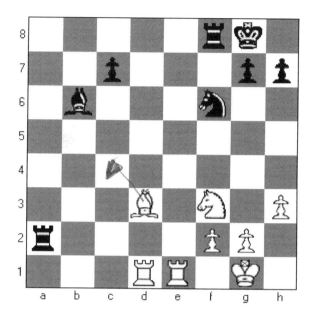

#21

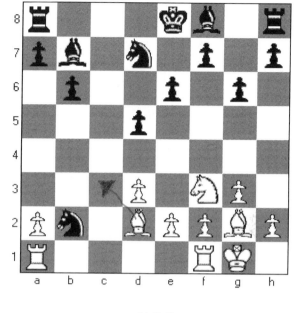

#22

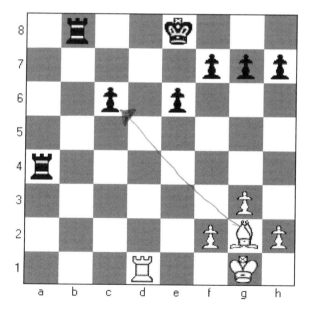

#23

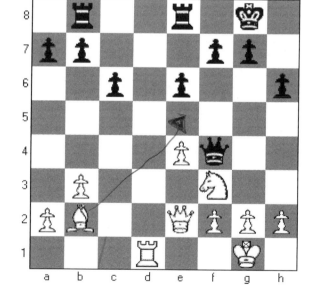

#24

Double Attacks-Rooks

Draw an arrow to show how White can use a double attack to win material

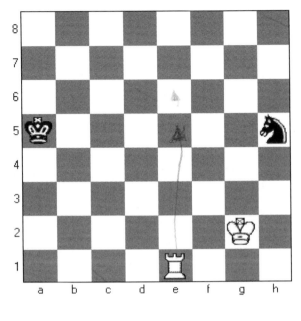

#25

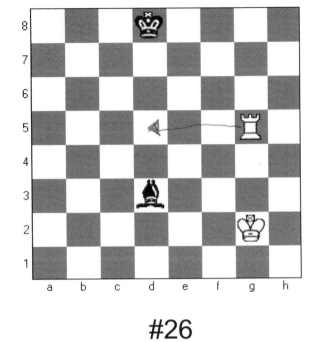

#26

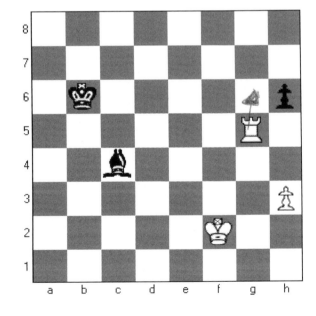

#27

#28

Double Attacks-Rooks

Draw an arrow to show how White can use a double attack to win material

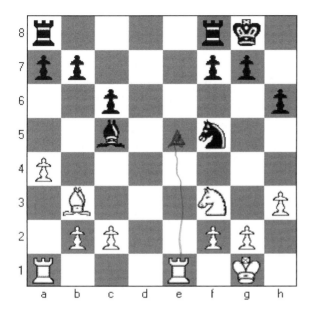

#29

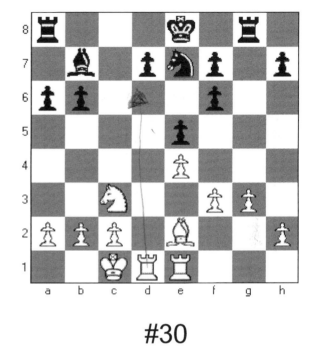

#30

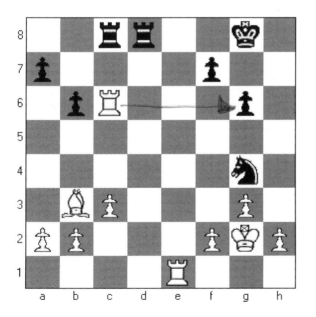

#31

#32

Double Attacks-Queens

Draw an arrow to show how White can use a double attack to win material

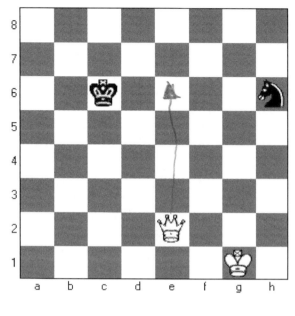

#33

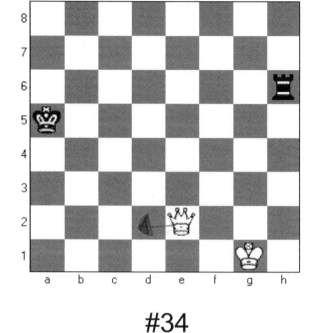

#34

#35

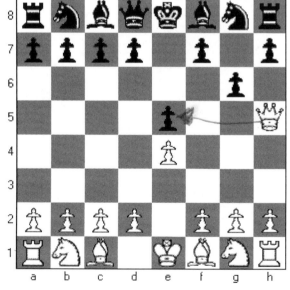

#36

Double Attacks-Queens

Draw an arrow to show how White can use a double attack to win material

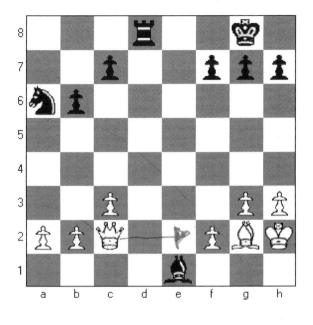

#37

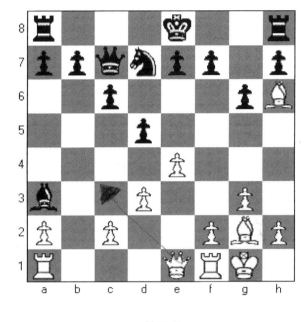

#38

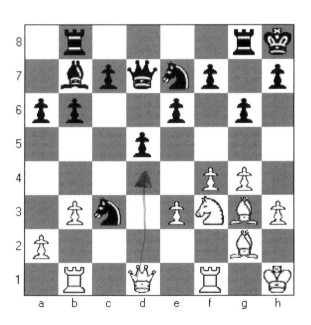

#39

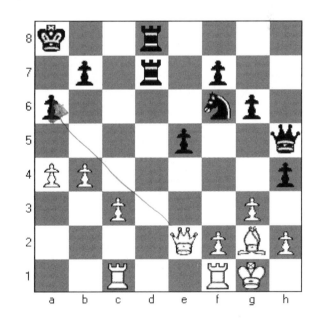

#40

Double Attacks-Kings

Draw an arrow to show how White can use a double attack to win material

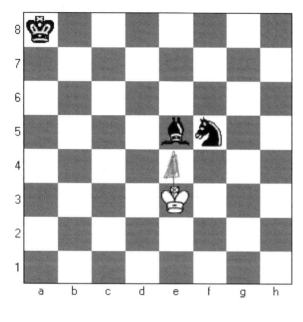

#41

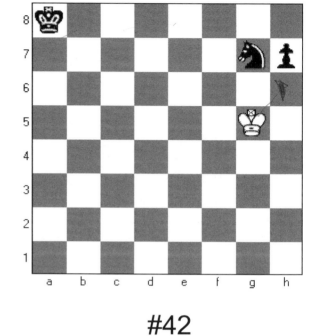

#42

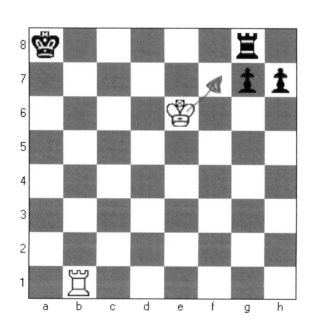

#43

#44

Double Attacks-1 move

Draw an arrow to show how White can use a double attack to win material

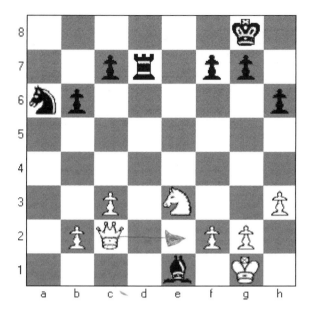

#45

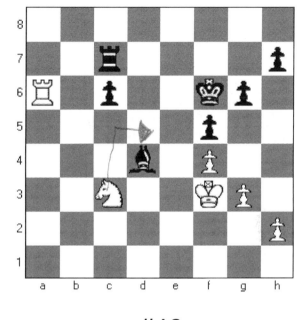

#46

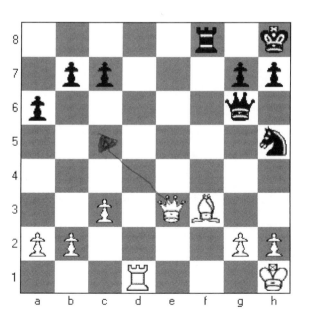

#47

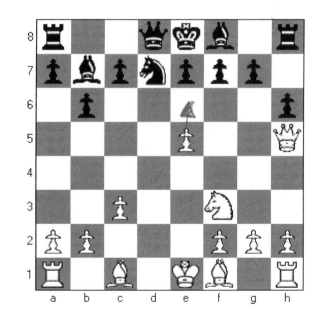

#48

Double Attacks-1 move

Draw an arrow to show how White can use a double attack to win material

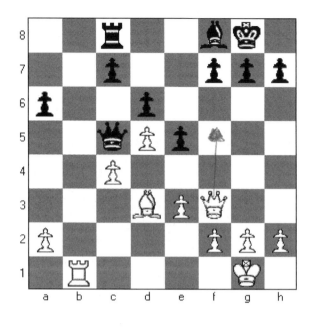

#49

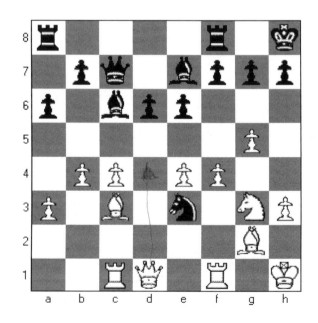

#50

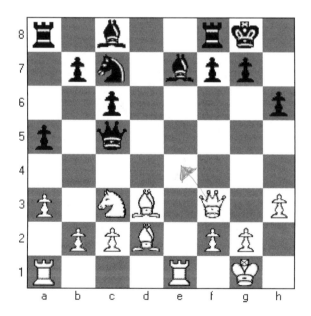

#51

#52

Double Attacks-2 moves

Draw an arrow or use chess notation to show how White can use a
double attack to win material

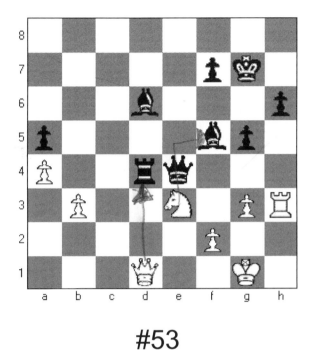

#53

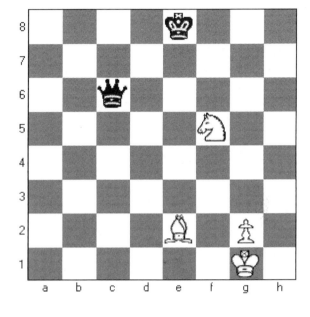

#54

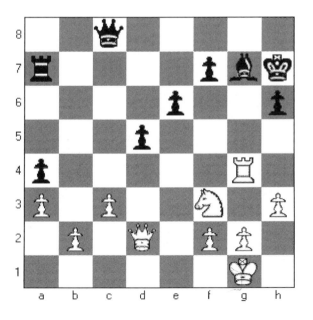

#55

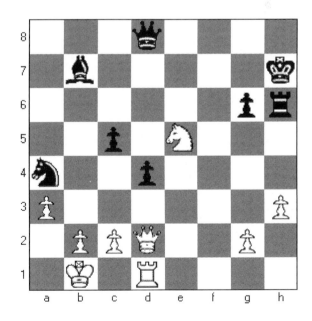

#56

Double Attacks-2 moves

Draw an arrow or use chess notation to show how White can use a
double attack to win material

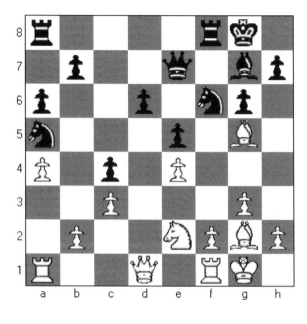

#57

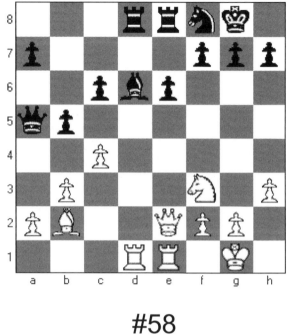

#58

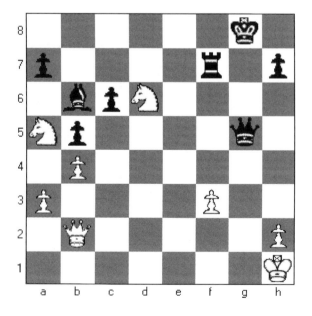

#59

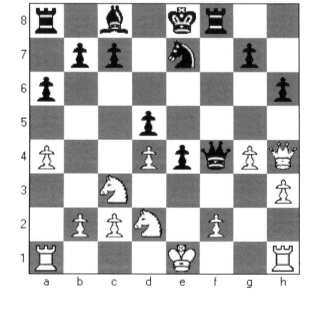

#60

Double Attacks-2 moves

Draw an arrow or use chess notation to show how White can use a
double attack to win material

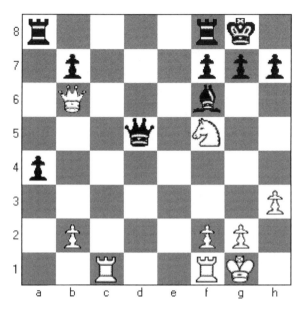

#61

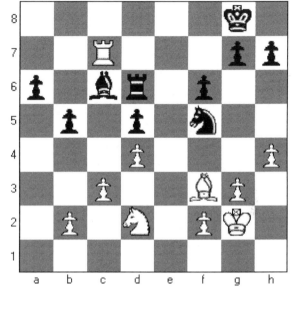

#62

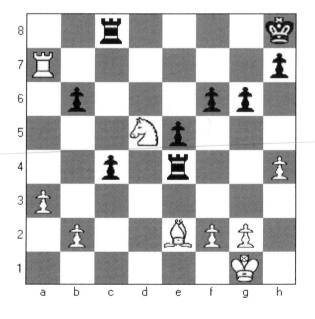

#63

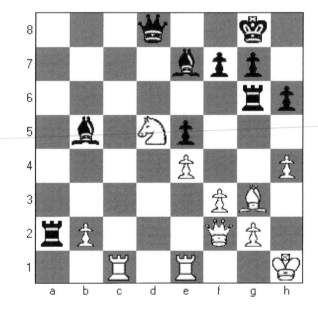

#64

Double Attacks-2 moves

Draw an arrow or use chess notation to show how White can use a
double attack to win material

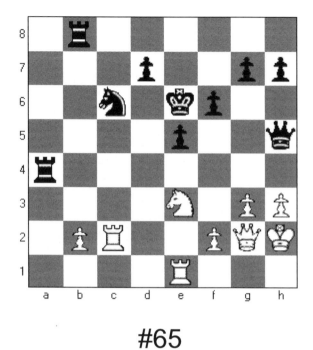

#65

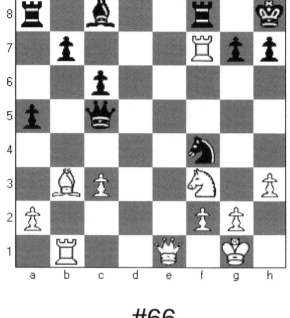

#66

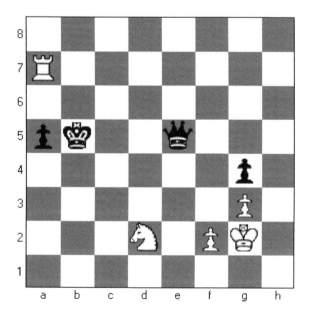

#67

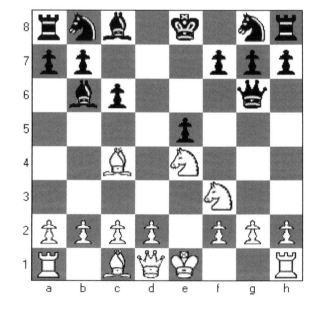

#68

Double Attacks-2 moves

Draw an arrow or use chess notation to show how White can use a
double attack to win material

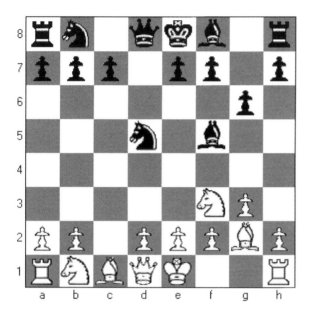

#69

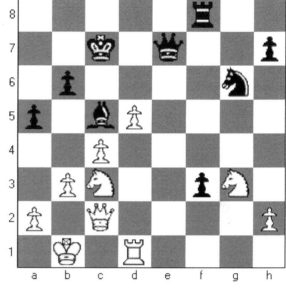

#70

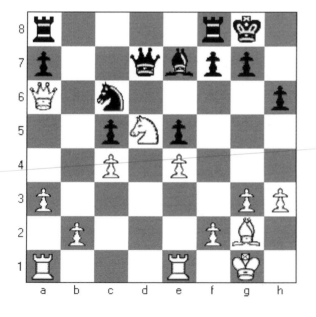

#71

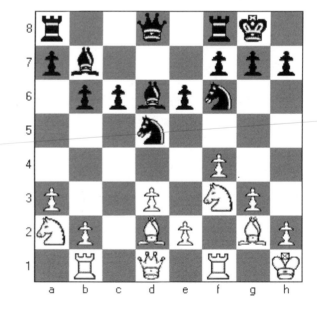

#72

Double Attacks-2 moves

Draw an arrow or use chess notation to show how White can use a
double attack to win material

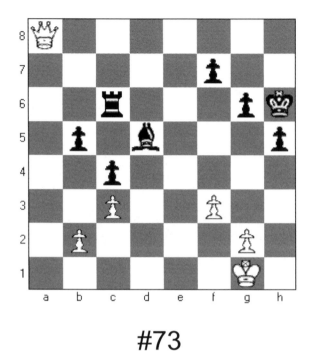

#73

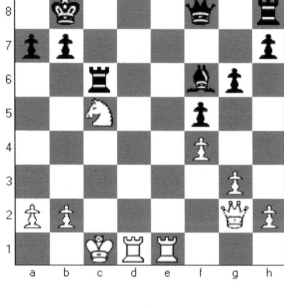

#74

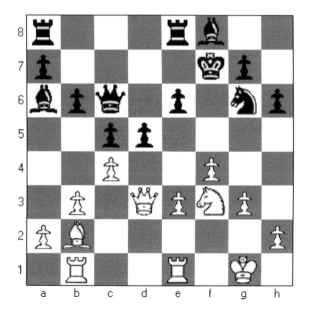

#75

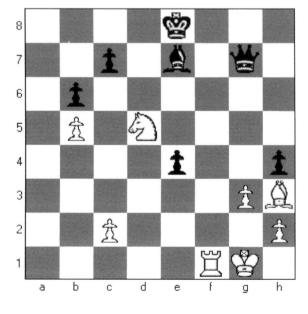

#76

Double Attacks-3 moves or more!

Use chess notation to show how White can use a double attack to win material

#77

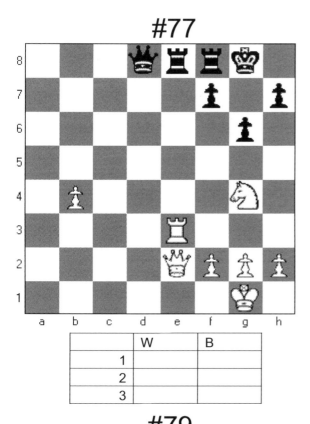

	W	B
1		
2		
3		

#78

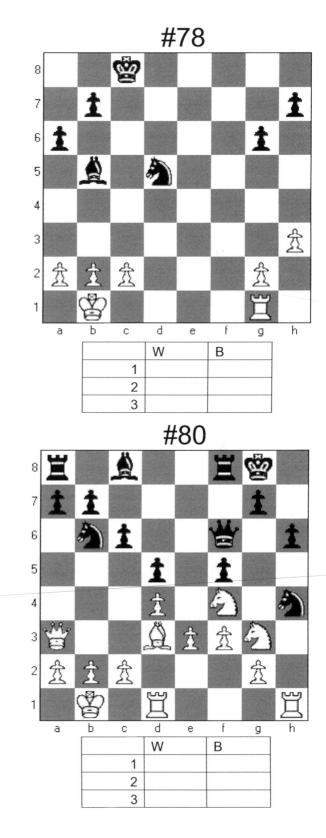

	W	B
1		
2		
3		

#79

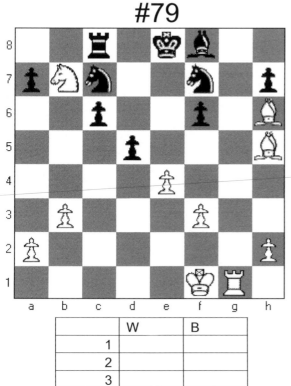

	W	B
1		
2		
3		

#80

	W	B
1		
2		
3		

Double Attacks-3 moves or more!

Use chess notation to show how White can use a double attack to win material

#81

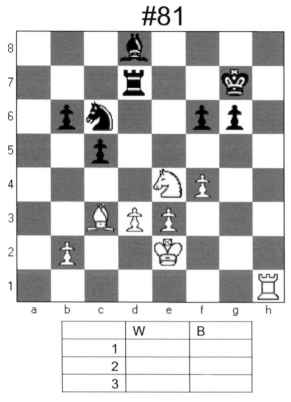

	W	B
1		
2		
3		

#82

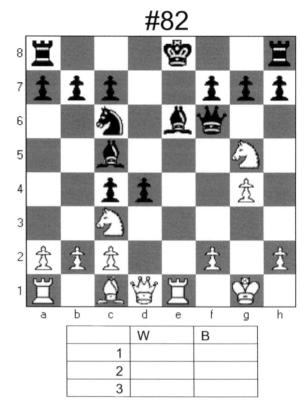

	W	B
1		
2		
3		

#83

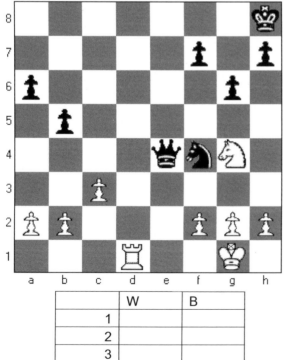

	W	B
1		
2		
3		

#84

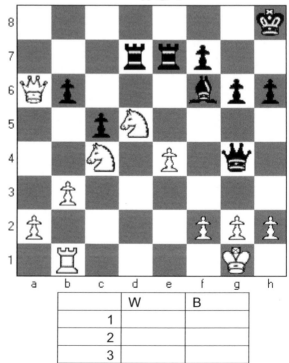

	W	B
1		
2		
3		

Double Attacks-3 moves or more!

Use chess notation to show how White can use a double attack to win material

#85

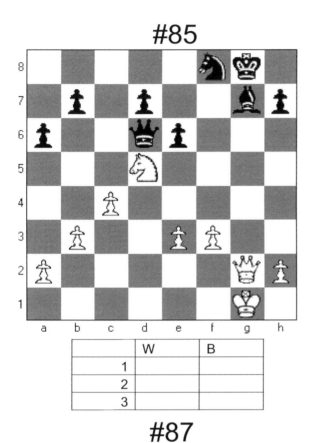

	W	B
1		
2		
3		

#86

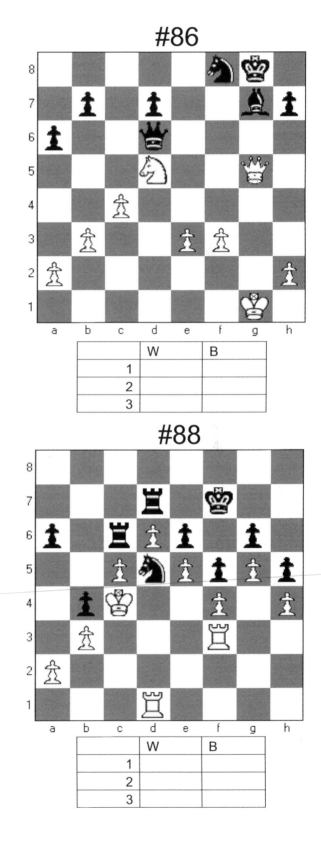

	W	B
1		
2		
3		

#87

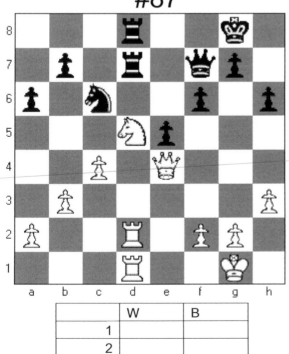

	W	B
1		
2		
3		

#88

	W	B
1		
2		
3		

Double Attacks-3 moves or more!

Use chess notation to show how White can use a double attack to win material

#89

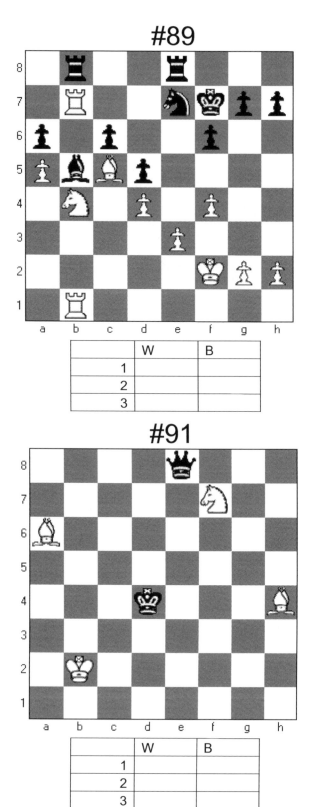

	W	B
1		
2		
3		

#90

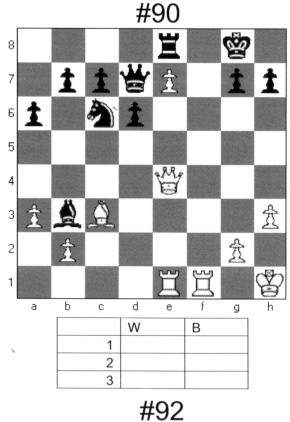

	W	B
1		
2		
3		

#91

	W	B
1		
2		
3		
4		

#92

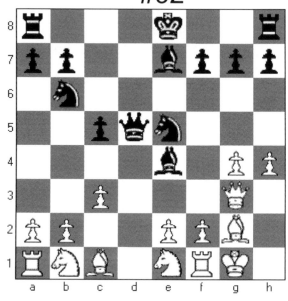

?

Chess Tactics-Remove the Guard & Deflection

Many times our opponent will stop one of our threats by using a guard. If this happens we can use one of two chess tactics. We can either try to **remove the guard** or use **deflection**. Removing the guard involves **capturing** the guard which then allows us to affect our threat. The other tactic is **deflection**. In this, we look to deflect or move that guard someplace where it does not defend our threat. Let us first look at some simple examples.

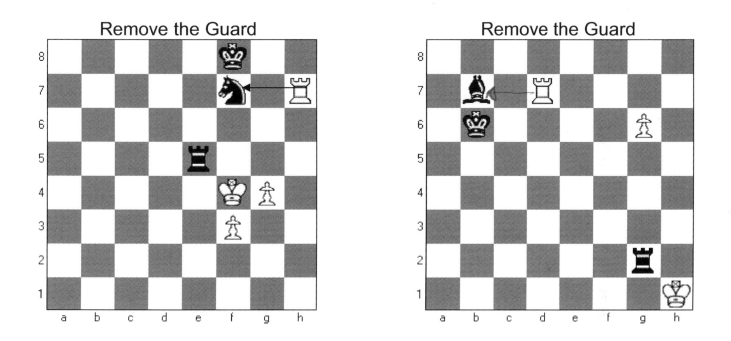

In the first diagram, White would be very happy if he could capture Black's rook. The problem is that the Black rook has a guard, the knight. If White can remove the guard from the rook, he will be able to capture it.

Q: Can White remove the guard?

A: Yes, the White rook can first capture the Black knight, and then the White king will be free to capture the Black rook next turn.

In the second diagram, the Black bishop is protecting the Black rook. The bishop is the guard. If White can remove the guard, then his king can capture Black's rook. Can you figure out how to remove the guard?

Chess Tactics

Let's see if you figured it out.

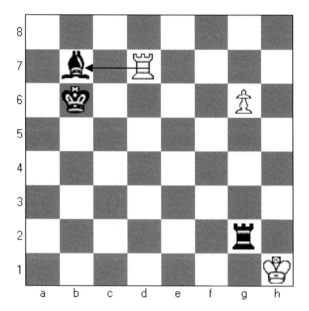

First, the White rook can capture the Black bishop.

The Black king can then capture the White rook.

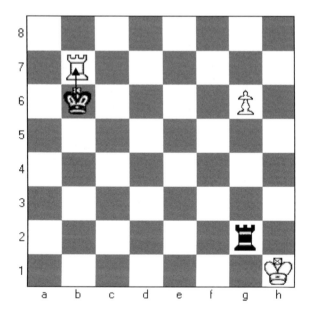

Since there is no more guard protecting the Black rook, the White king can capture it.

White lost a rook in the above position. Q: What did he gain?

A: White gained a rook and a bishop. So he was able to use the **remove the guard** tactic to gain material.

Chess Tactics

Let's see a simple example of deflection

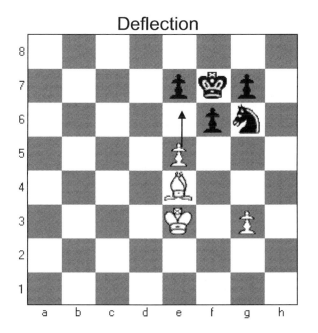

Deflection

Here, White wants to capture the Black knight. However, the knight is defended by the Black king. White can **deflect** the Black king by moving his pawn up to e6 to check the Black king. The Black king will have to move away from the defense of his knight by either capturing the White pawn or moving backward. Once that happens, White can safely capture the Black knight. White was able to remove the guard (the king) by using deflection.

So we see that the remove the guard and deflection tactics are very similar. Now let's try the problems.

Remove the Guard & Deflection

Draw an arrow or use chess notation to show how White can remove the guard or use deflection to win material or more

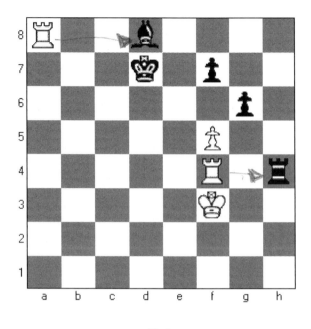

#1

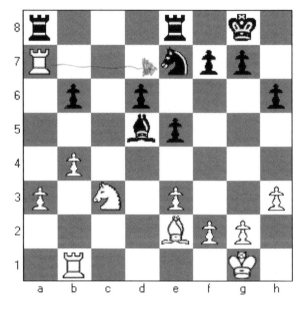

#2

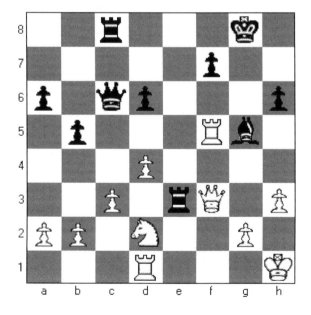

#3

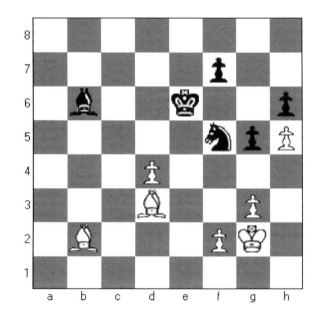

#4

Remove the Guard & Deflection

Draw an arrow or use chess notation to show how White can remove the guard or use deflection to win material or more

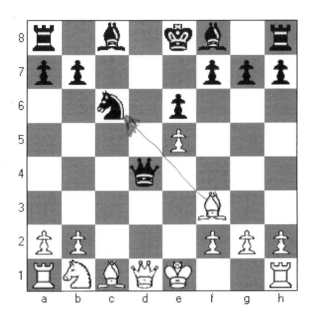

#5

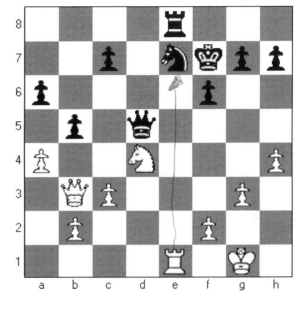

#6

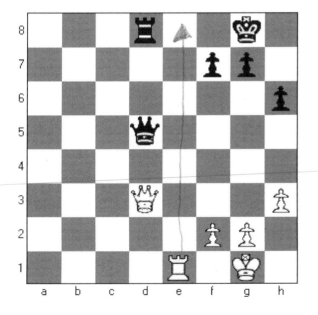

#7

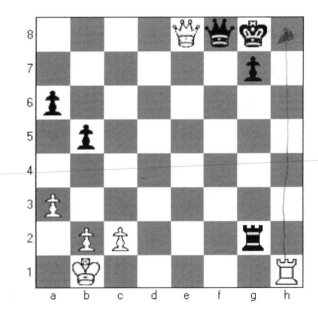

#8

Remove the Guard & Deflection

Draw an arrow or use chess notation to show how White can remove the guard or use deflection to win material or more

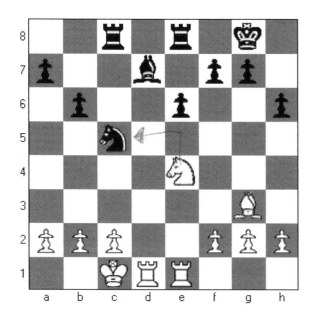

#9

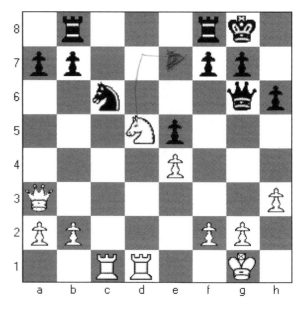

#10

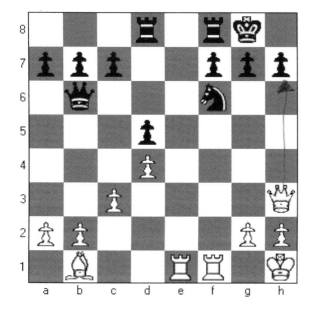

#11

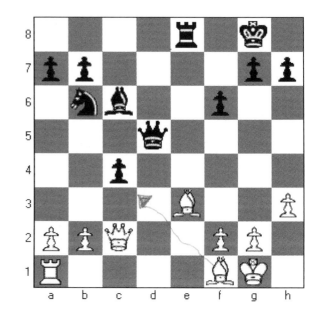

#12

Remove the Guard & Deflection-Difficult!

Draw an arrow or use chess notation to show how White can remove the guard or use deflection to win material or more

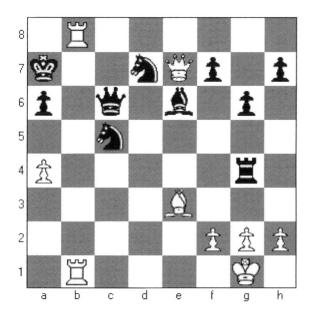

#13

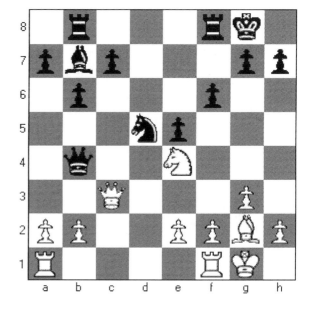

#14

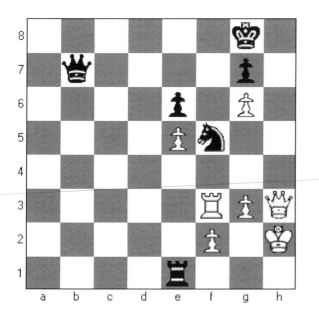

#15

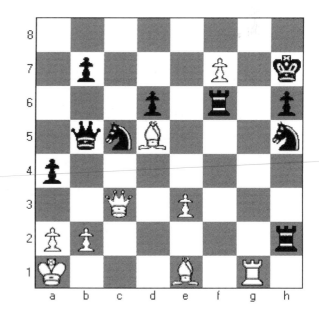

#16

Chess Tactics-Pin

Another chess tactic is the **pin**. A pin is when you use one of your pieces to attack one of your opponent's less valuable pieces, and if that less valuable piece moves, a bigger piece is in danger. You can pin a piece to a piece, but you can also pin a piece to a threat, like checkmate. Below is an example:

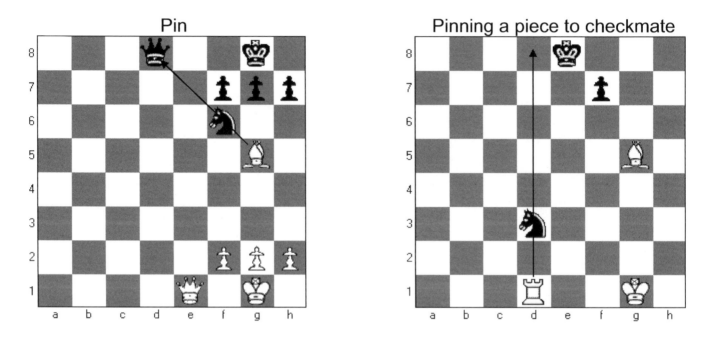

In the first diagram, the White bishop attacks the Black knight. If the Black knight (the less valuable piece) moves, the Black queen (the more valuable piece) can be captured.

In the second diagram, the White rook pins the Black knight to a threat. That threat is checkmate. If the Black knight moves, the White rook will move to d8 and checkmate the Black king.

Q: Why can't the Black king capture the White rook?

A: The bishop is protecting the rook.

So we can see that pins are when you attack a smaller piece and that piece doesn't want to (or can't) move out of the way because something worse will happen.

Chess Tactics

Let's quickly look at some simple pins together.

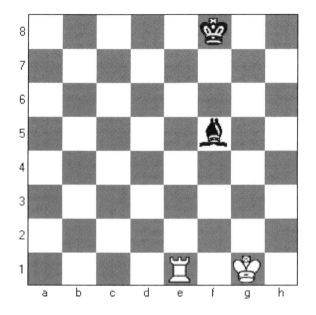

Q: Can the White rook move someplace to pin the Black bishop to the Black king?

A: The White rook can move to f1 where it attacks the Black bishop. The Black bishop cannot move, since the Black king would then be in danger. This is a special type of pin called an **absolute pin.** That means that the bishop cannot make any legal moves since it cannot expose the Black king to danger.

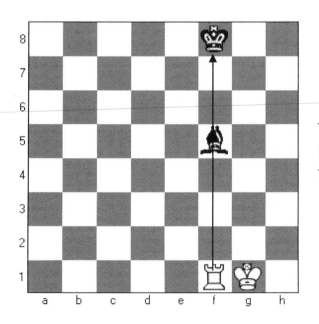

There is no way that Black can save the bishop. White will capture it on his next turn.

Chess Tactics

Sometimes you have already successfully pinned a piece. What should you do once you have pinned a piece? You should try to capture it! But what if it is protected? Keep in mind that a pinned piece does not want to move. It is stuck! So you want to attack it!

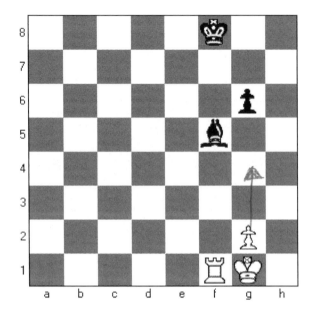

Now the bishop is still caught in an absolute pin. However, if White captures it now with his rook, Black will capture back with his pawn.

Q: So what should White do?

A: White can use the pin to win the bishop anyway.

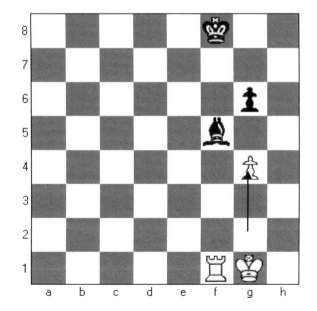

After White moves his g-pawn to g4, Black's bishop is threatened by the pawn. The poor Black bishop cannot save himself because he cannot move.

Tip: Attack pieces that are pinned with your smallest possible piece! Attacking pinned pieces with pawns is usually the most effective way of using a pin to win material.

Pins-1 move

Draw an arrow to show how White can use a pin to win material

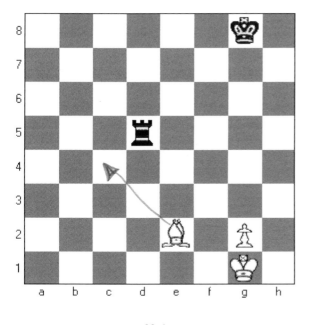

#1

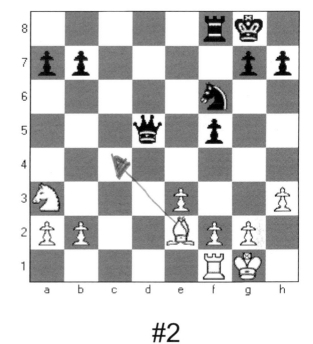

#2

#3

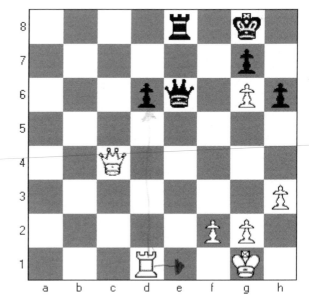

#4

Pins-1 move

Draw an arrow to show how White can use a pin to win material or more

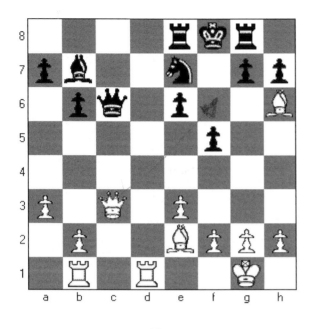

#5

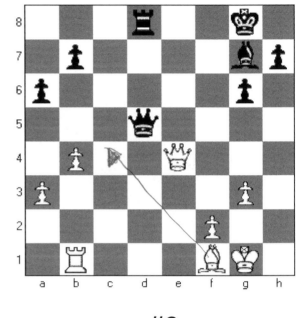

#6

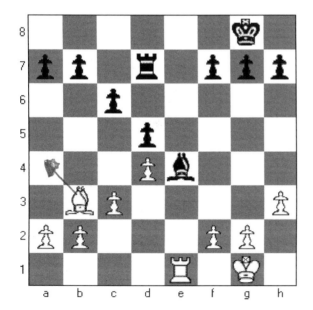

#7

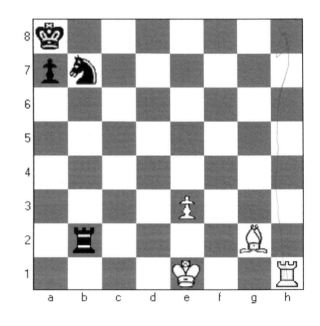

#8

Pins-2 moves

Draw an arrow or use chess notation to show how White can use a pin
to win material

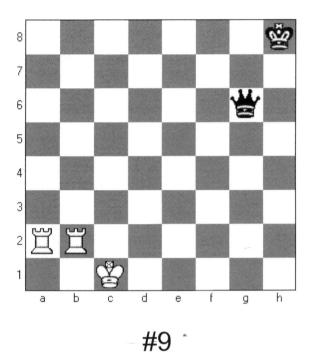

#9

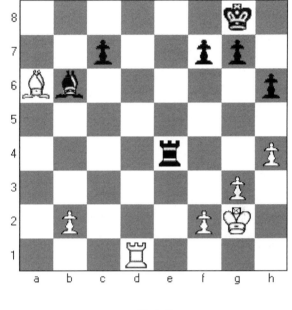

#10

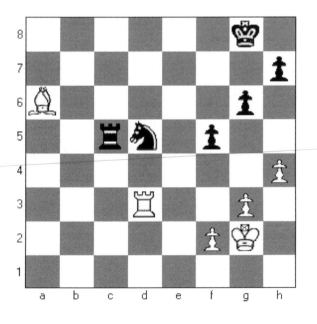

#11

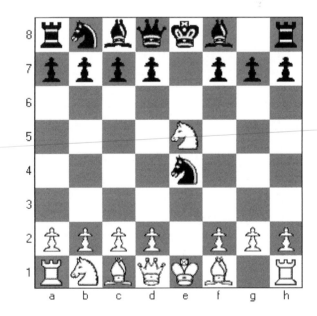

#12

Pins-2 moves-Difficult!

Draw an arrow or use chess notation to show how White can use a pin
to win material or more

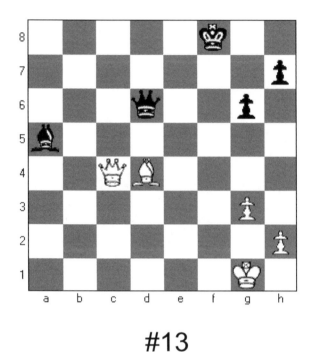

#13

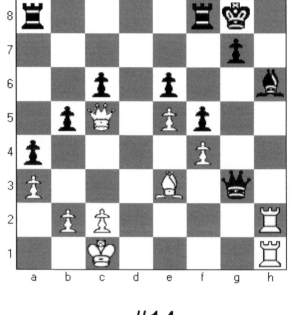

#14

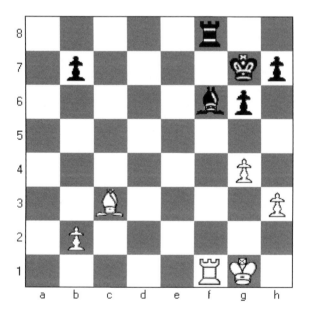

#15

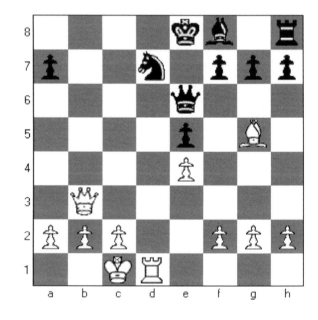

#16

Chess Tactics-Skewer

Yet another chess tactic is the **skewer**. A skewer is the opposite of a pin. In a pin, the less valuable piece is in front of the more valuable piece. In a skewer, the more valuable piece is in front of the less valuable piece. Let's look at some examples.

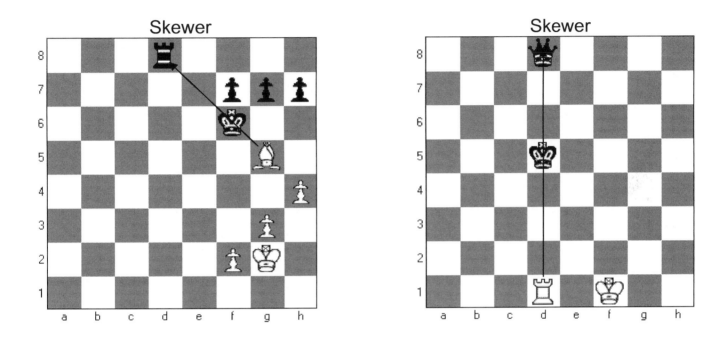

In the first diagram, the White bishop attacks the Black king. When the Black king (the more valuable piece) moves, the Black rook (the less valuable piece) can be captured.

In the second diagram, the White rook skewers the Black king to the Black queen. When the Black king moves, the White rook will capture the Black queen.

Now, let's do some exercises together!

Chess Tactics

Let's quickly look at an obvious skewer.

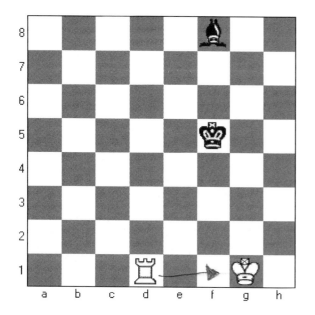

Q: Can the White rook move someplace to skewer the Black king to the Black bishop?

A: The White rook can move to f1 where it attacks the Black king. When the Black king moves, the bishop will be captured.

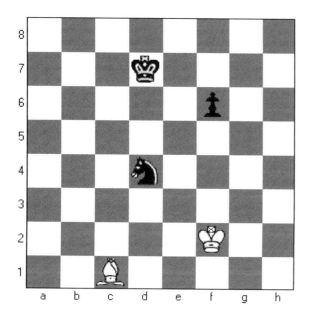

Here is a skewer using smaller pieces. If the White bishop moves to b2, it will skewer the knight to the pawn. The more valuable piece (the knight) is in line with the less valuable piece (the pawn). Don't forget that even skewers that win a pawn are important!

Skewers-1 move

Draw an arrow to show how White can use a skewer to win material

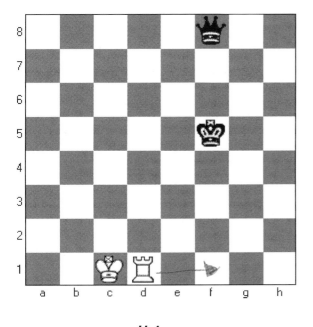

#1

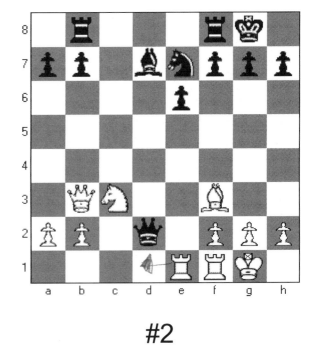

#2

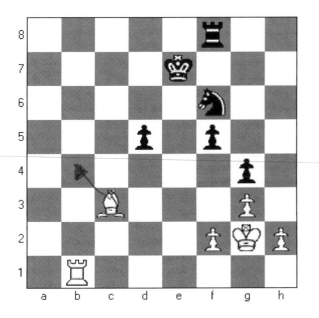

#3

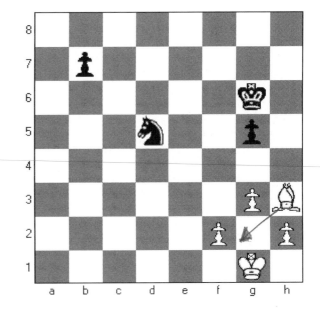

#4

Skewers-2 moves

Draw an arrow to show how White can use a skewer to win material

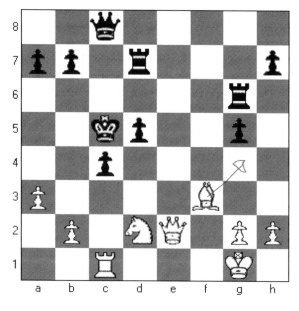

#5

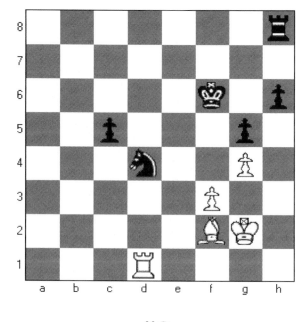

#6

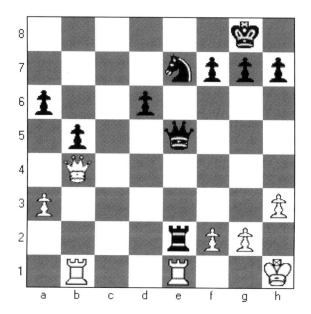

#7

#8

Chapter 3-Checkmate in 2 Moves

From this chapter through the rest of the book, strategies will progressively get more difficult. Here, you will need to find a way to FORCE checkmate in 2 moves. That means that you will make a move, your opponent will respond with a move, and then your second move MUST be checkmate. You must choose your opponent's best move. For example, you can't make a bad move for your opponent just to be able to make checkmate. The first problems will be regular checkmate in 2 problems. Look at the most forcing moves first (the checks) and this will greatly help your chances of finding the solution. The next sections in the chapter will provide a hint such as checkmate in 2 using the remove the guard idea that we learned about in the last chapter. This chapter will take longer than the previous chapters. Our master can complete this chapter successfully in 30 minutes. A good time estimate to solve this entire section is an hour and a half.

Good luck!

Mate in 2

Draw arrows or use chess notation to show how White can checkmate in two moves

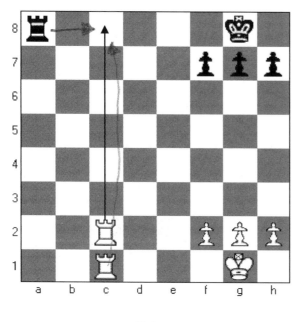

#1

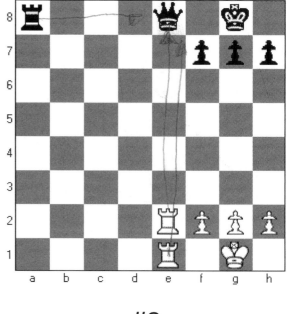

#2

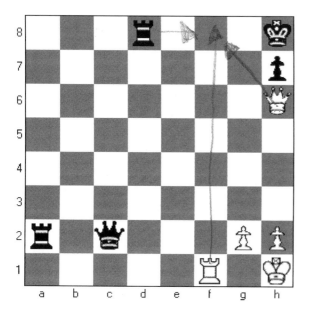

#3

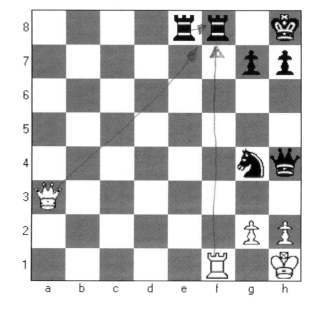

#4

Mate in 2

Draw arrows or use chess notation to show how White can checkmate in two moves

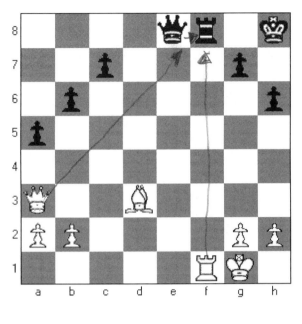

#5

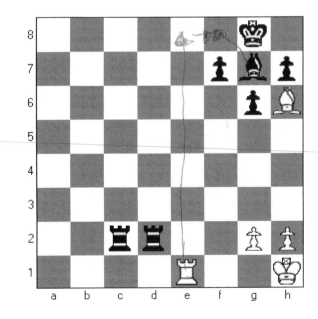

#6

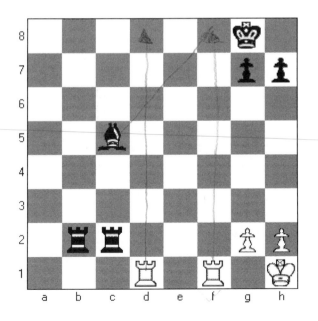

#7

#8

Mate in 2

Draw arrows or use chess notation to show how White can checkmate in two moves

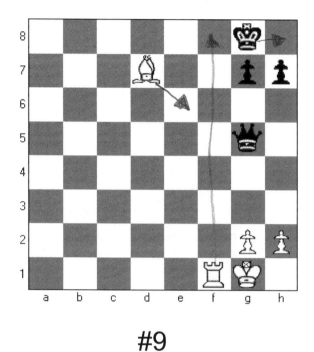

#9

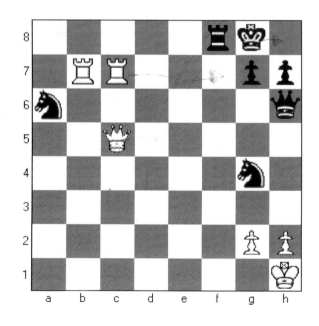

#10

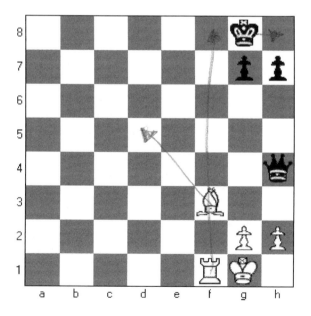

#11

#12

Mate in 2

Draw arrows or use chess notation to show how White can checkmate in two moves

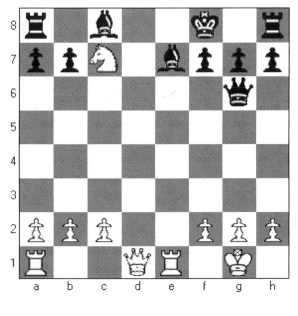

#13

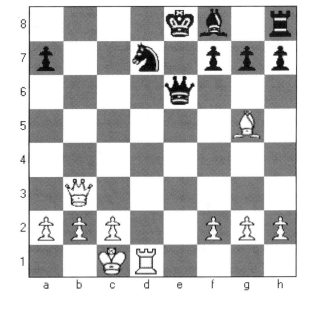

#14

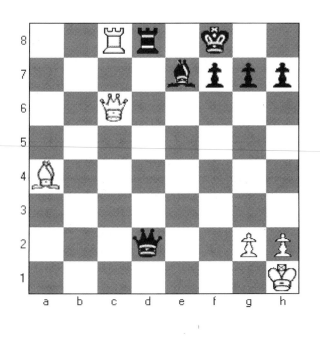

#15

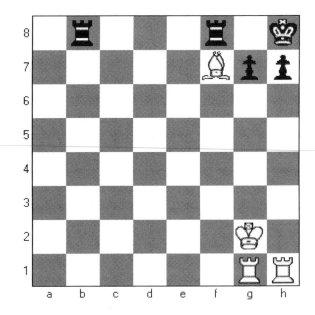

#16

Mate in 2

Draw arrows or use chess notation to show how White can checkmate in two moves

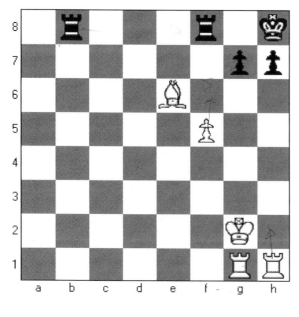

#17

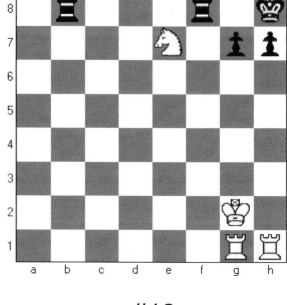

#18

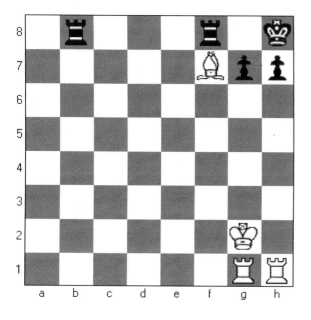

#19

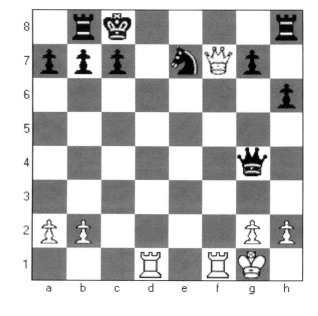

#20

Mate in 2

Draw arrows or use chess notation to show how White can checkmate in two moves

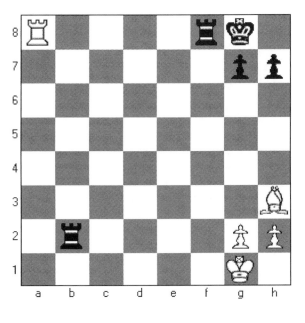

#21

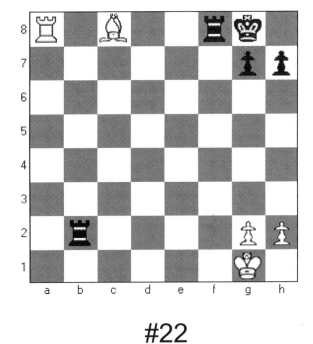

#22

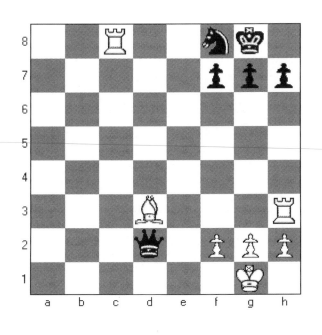

#23

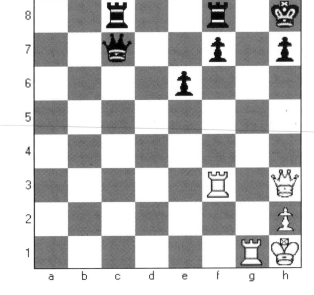

#24

Mate in 2

Draw arrows or use chess notation to show how White can checkmate in two moves

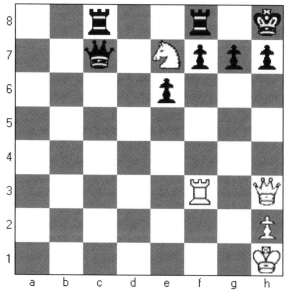

#25

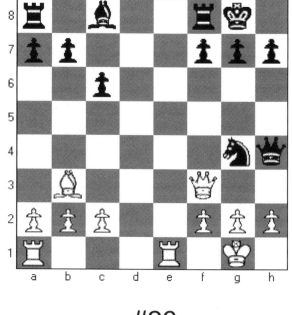

#26

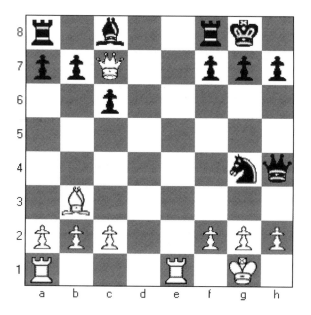

#27

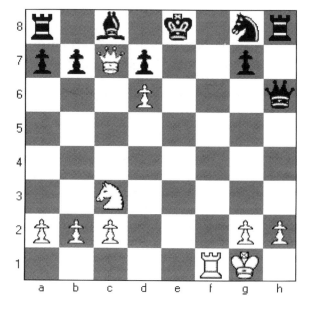

#28

Mate in 2

Draw arrows or use chess notation to show how White can checkmate in two moves

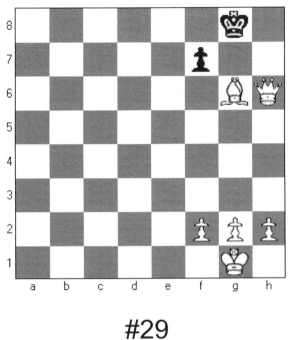

#29

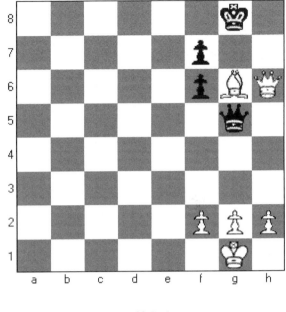

#30

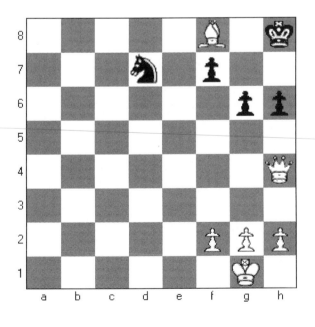

#31

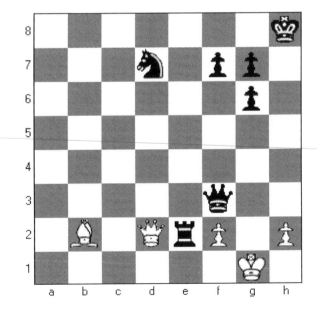

#32

Mate in 2

Draw arrows or use chess notation to show how White can checkmate in two moves

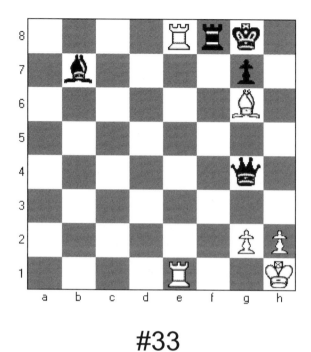

#33

#34

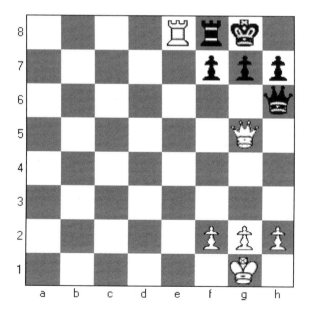

#35

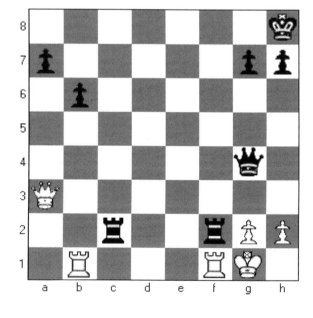

#36

Mate in 2

Draw arrows or use chess notation to show how White can checkmate in two moves

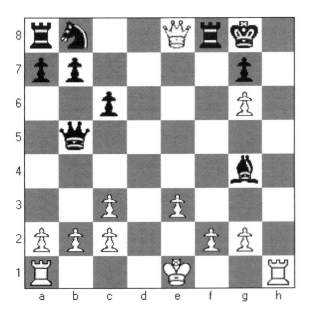

#37

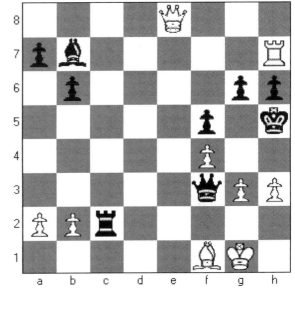

#38

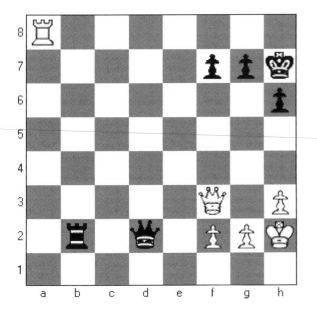

#39

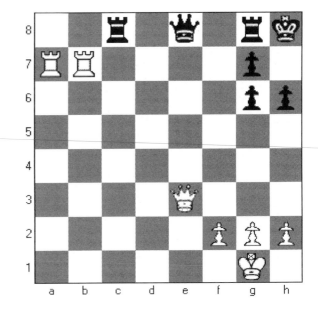

#40

Mate in 2

Draw arrows or use chess notation to show how White can checkmate in two moves

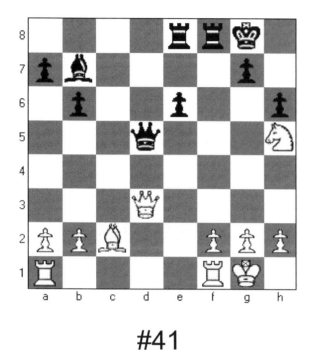

#41

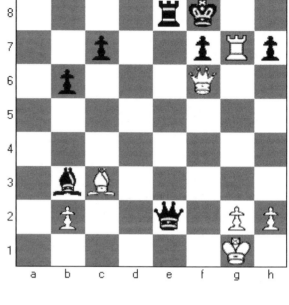

#42

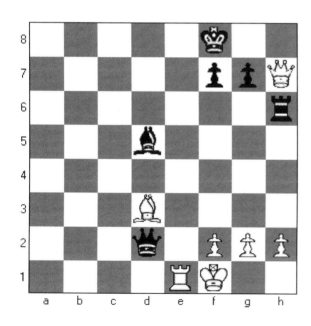

#43

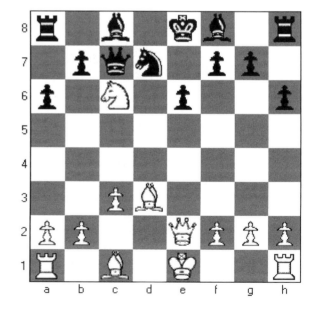

#44

Mate in 2-Remove the Guard & Deflection

Draw arrows or use chess notation to show how White can checkmate in two moves

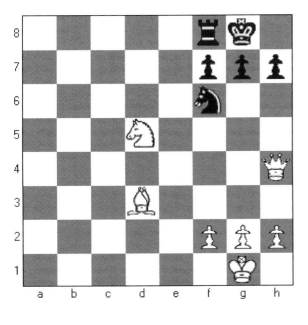

#45

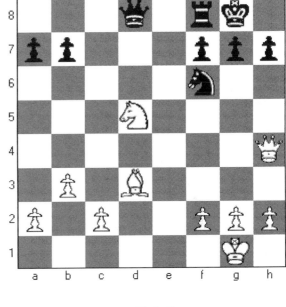

#46

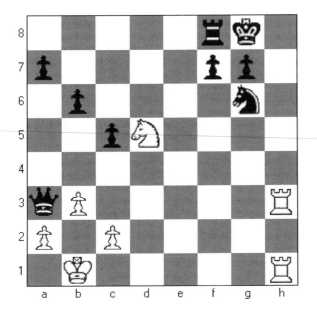

#47

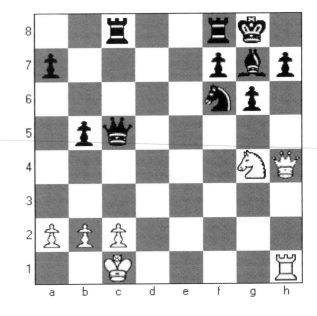

#48

Mate in 2-Remove the Guard & Deflection

Draw arrows or use chess notation to show how White can checkmate in two moves

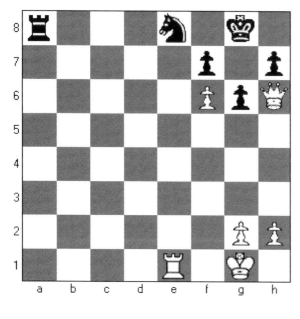

#49

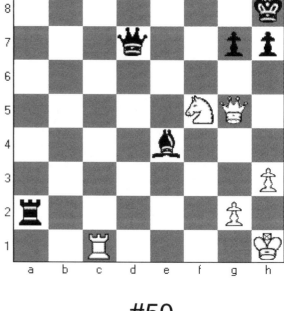

#50

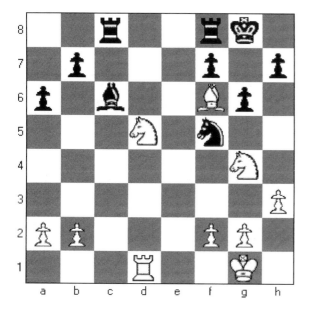

#51

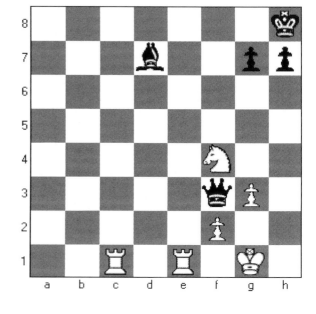

#52

Mate in 2-Remove the Guard & Deflection

Draw arrows or use chess notation to show how White can checkmate in two moves

#53

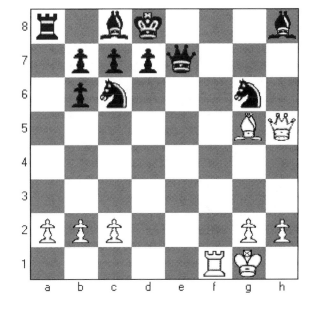

#54

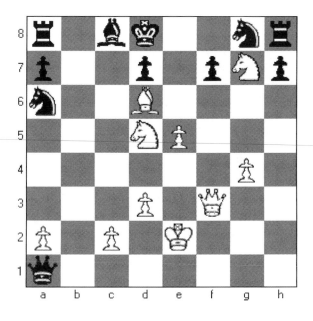

#55

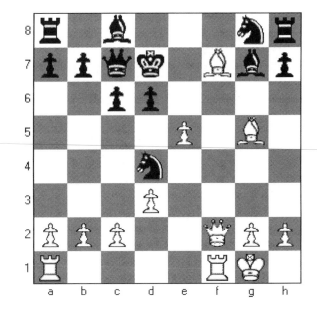

#56

Mate in 2-Remove the Guard & Deflection

Draw arrows or use chess notation to show how White can checkmate in two moves

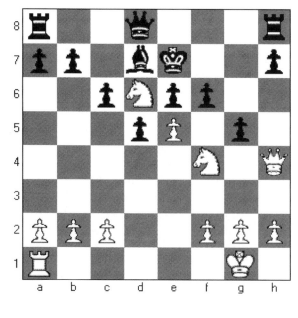

#57

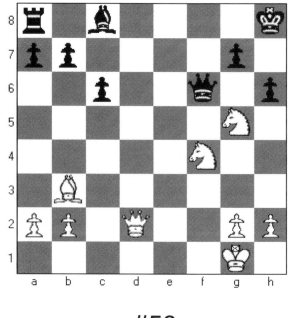

#58

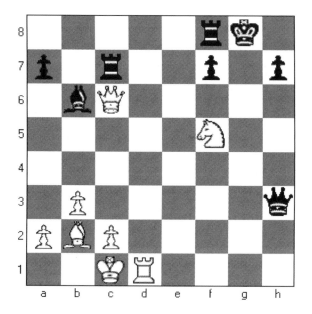

#59

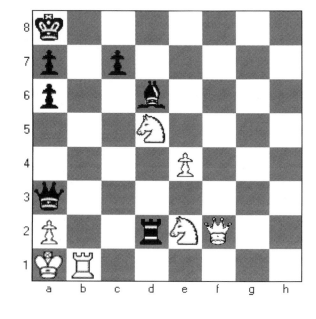

#60

Mate in 2-Remove the Guard & Deflection

Draw arrows or use chess notation to show how White can checkmate in two moves

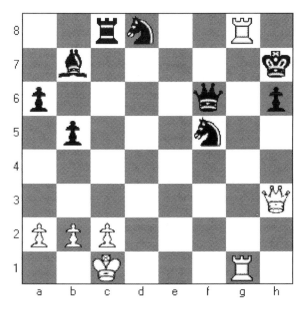

#61

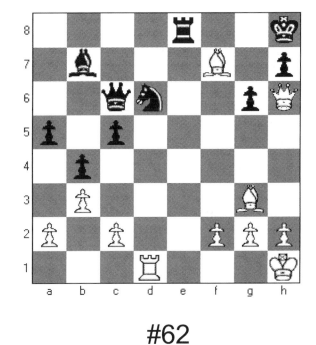

#62

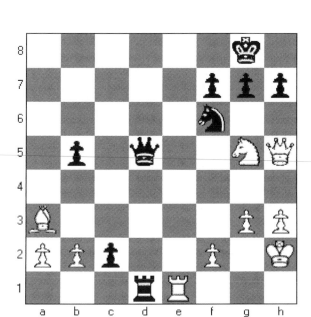

#63

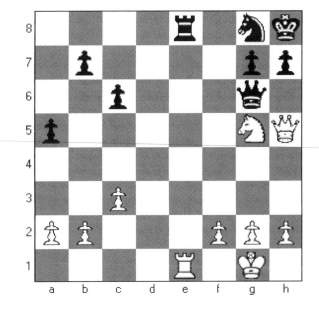

#64

Mate in 2-Square Clearance

Draw arrows or use chess notation to show how White can checkmate in two moves

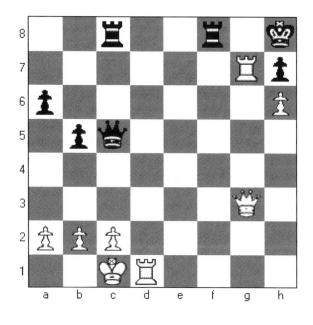

#65

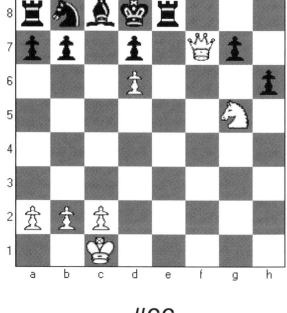

#66

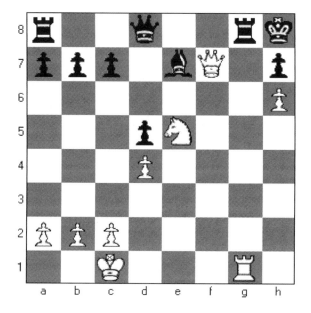

#67

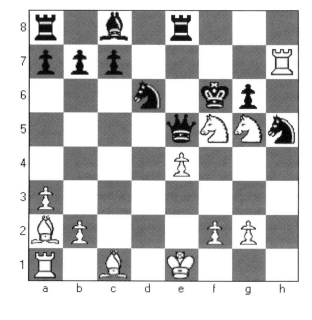

#68

Mate in 2-Square Clearance

Draw arrows or use chess notation to show how White can checkmate in two moves

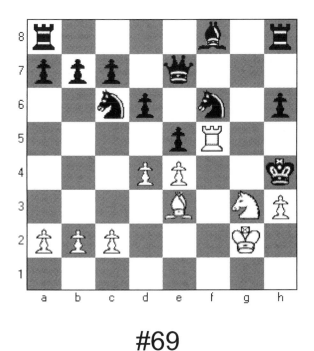

#69

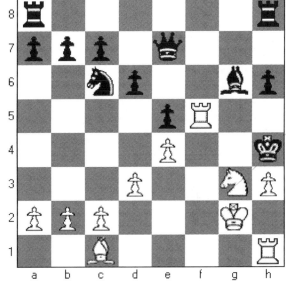

#70

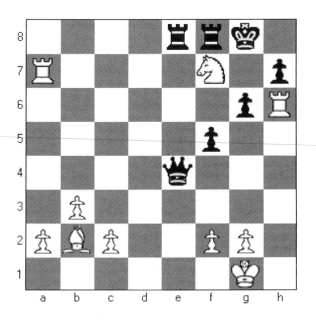

#71

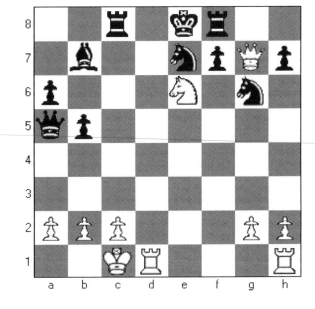

#72

Mate in 2-Queen and Helper

Draw arrows or use chess notation to show how White can checkmate in two moves

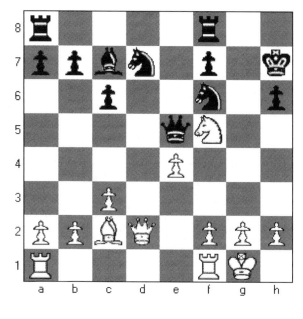

#73

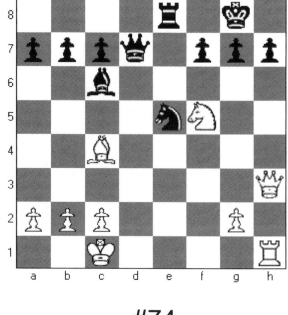

#74

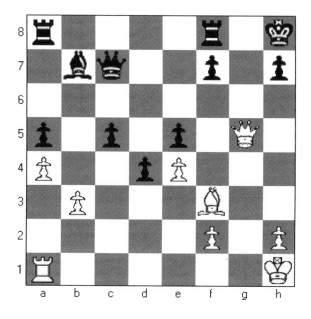

#75

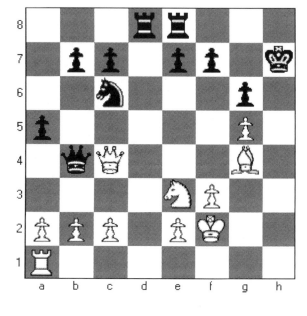

#76

Mate in 2-Queen and Helper

Draw arrows or use chess notation to show how White can checkmate in two moves

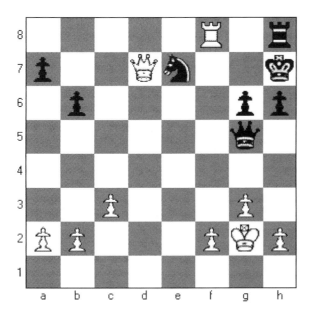

#77

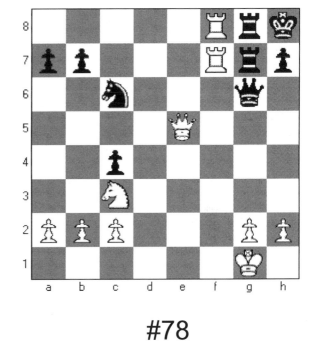

#78

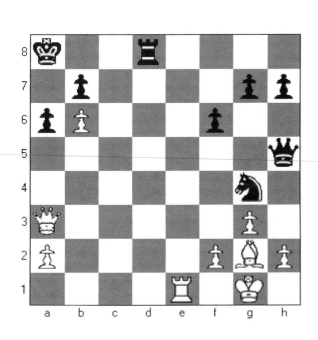

#79

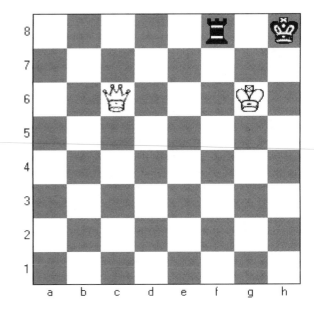

#80

Mate in 2-Difficult!

Draw arrows or use chess notation to show how White can checkmate in two moves

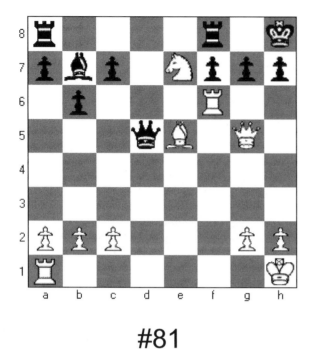

#81

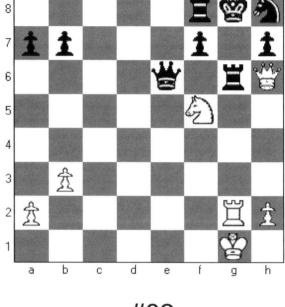

#82

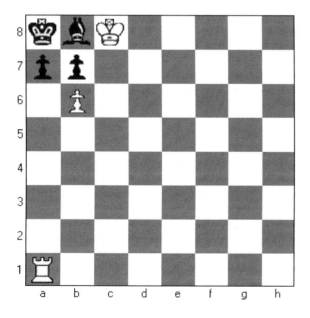

#83

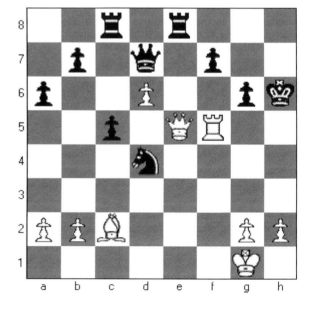

#84

Mate in 2-Difficult!

Draw arrows or use chess notation to show how White can checkmate in two moves

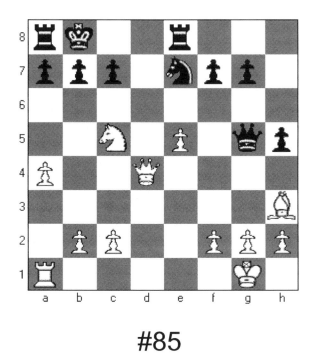

#85

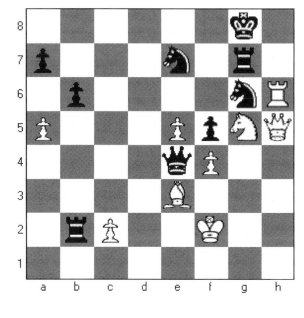

#86

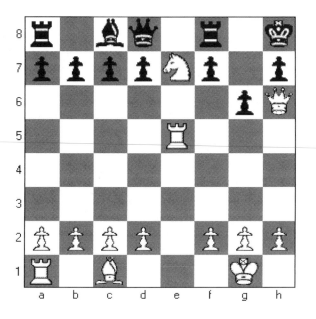

#87

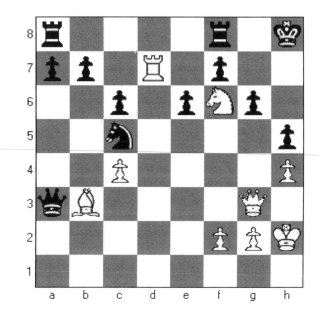

#88

Mate in 2-Difficult!

Draw arrows or use chess notation to show how White can checkmate in two moves

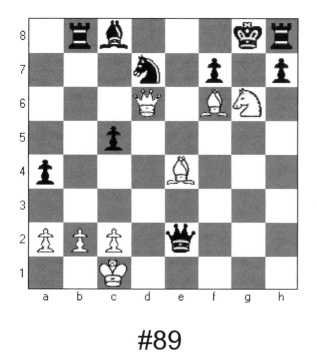

#89

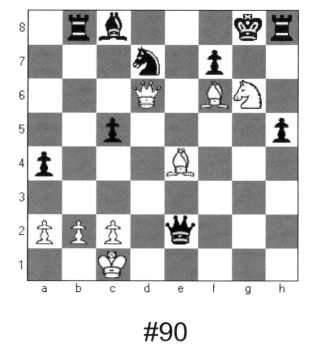

#90

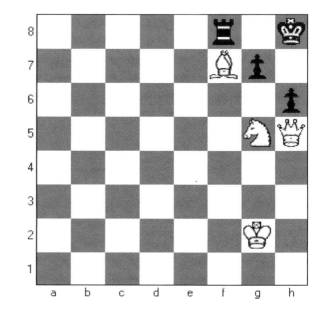

#91

#92

Mate in 2-Very Difficult!

Draw arrows or use chess notation to show how White can checkmate in two moves

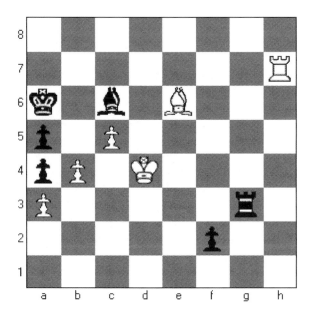

#93

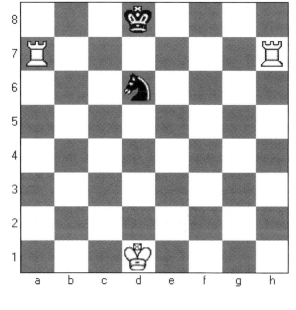

#94

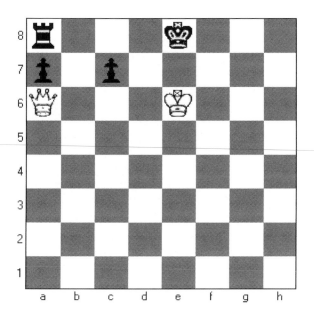

#95

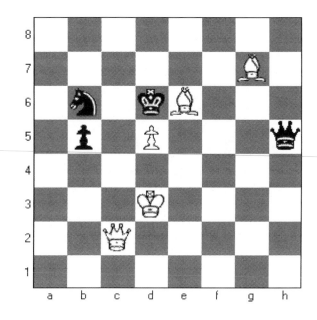

#96

Mate in 2-Very Difficult!

Draw arrows or use chess notation to show how White can checkmate in two moves

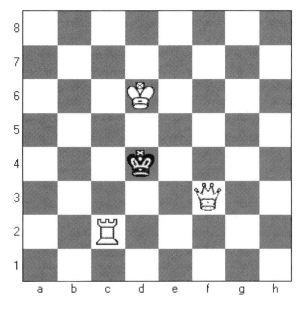

#97

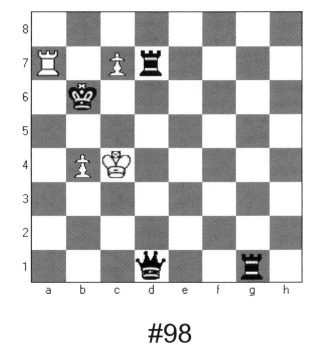

#98

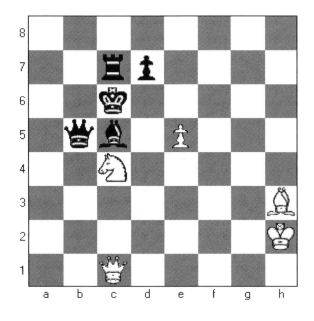

#99

#100

Chapter 4-Checkmate in 3 Moves

This section is challenging even for national champions. Unless instructed by your coach or teacher, you should not attempt this chapter until everything else before this has been mastered. In this chapter, you will also need to use chess notation to name the moves. You may want to review the chess notation section at the beginning of the workbook. Here, you will need to find a way to FORCE checkmate in 3 moves. Some pages will give a hint as to what type of theme to use. This section is very difficult and can even take experienced masters more than an hour to complete. Take your time on this section. It is more important to solve the problems than to do them quickly.

Good luck!

Mate in 3

Use chess notation to show how White can checkmate in three moves

#1

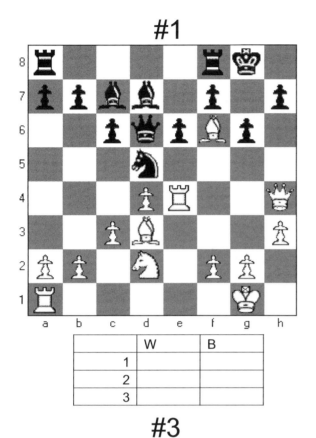

	W	B
1		
2		
3		

#2

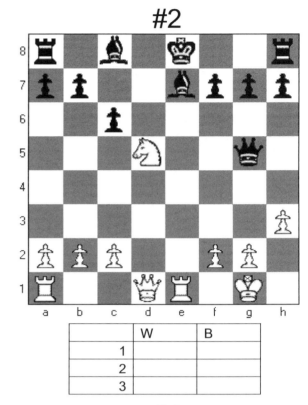

	W	B
1		
2		
3		

#3

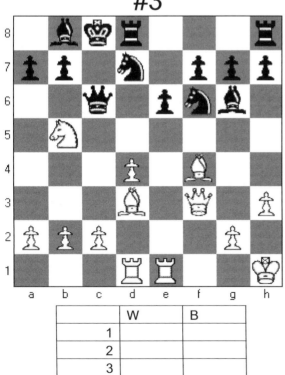

	W	B
1		
2		
3		

#4

	W	B
1		
2		
3		

Mate in 3

Use chess notation to show how White can checkmate in three moves

#5

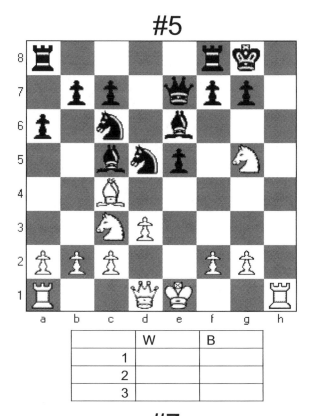

	W	B
1		
2		
3		

#6

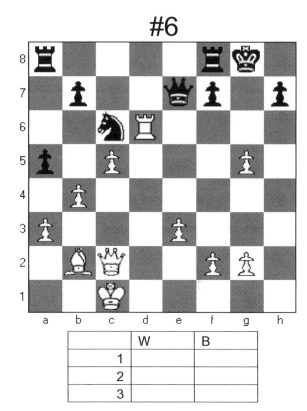

	W	B
1		
2		
3		

#7

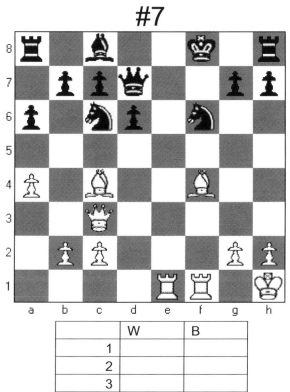

	W	B
1		
2		
3		

#8

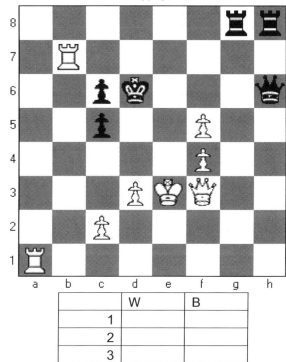

	W	B
1		
2		
3		

Mate in 3

Use chess notation to show how White can checkmate in three moves

#9

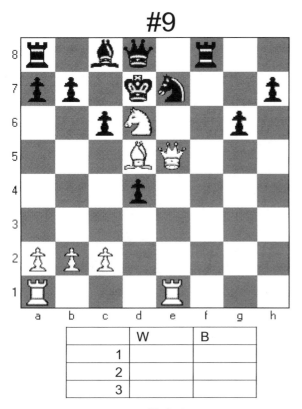

	W	B
1		
2		
3		

#10

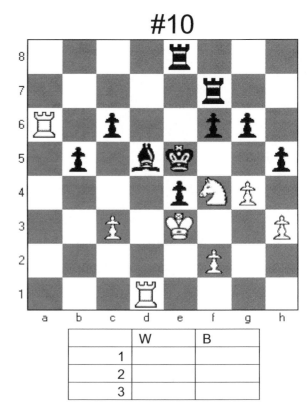

	W	B
1		
2		
3		

#11

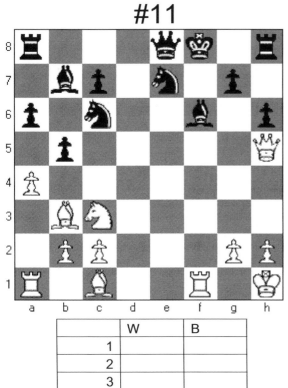

	W	B
1		
2		
3		

#12

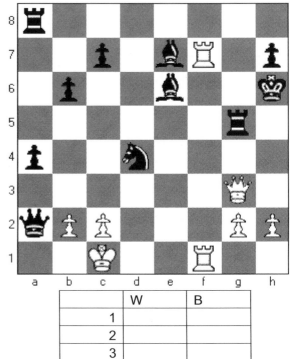

	W	B
1		
2		
3		

Mate in 3

Use chess notation to show how White can checkmate in three moves

#13

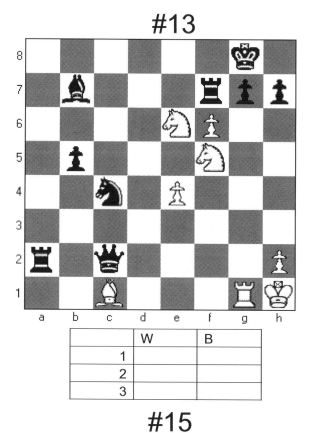

	W	B
1		
2		
3		

#14

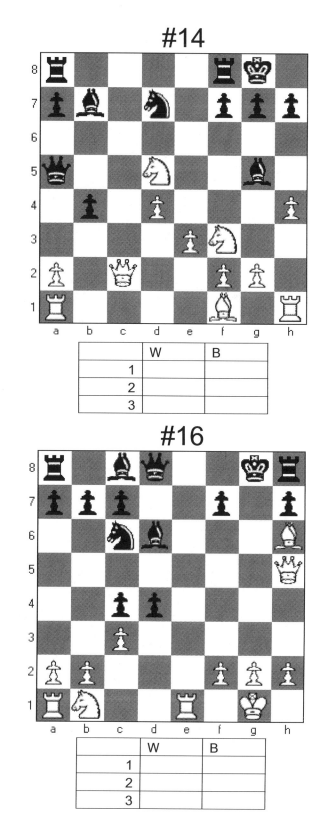

	W	B
1		
2		
3		

#15

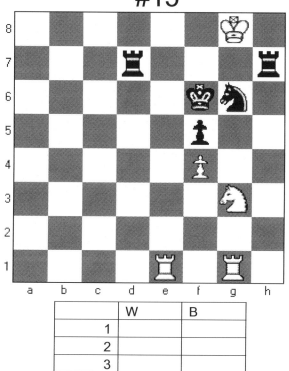

	W	B
1		
2		
3		

#16

	W	B
1		
2		
3		

Mate in 3

Use chess notation to show how White can checkmate in three moves

#17

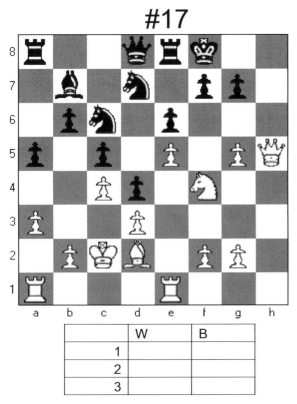

	W	B
1		
2		
3		

#18

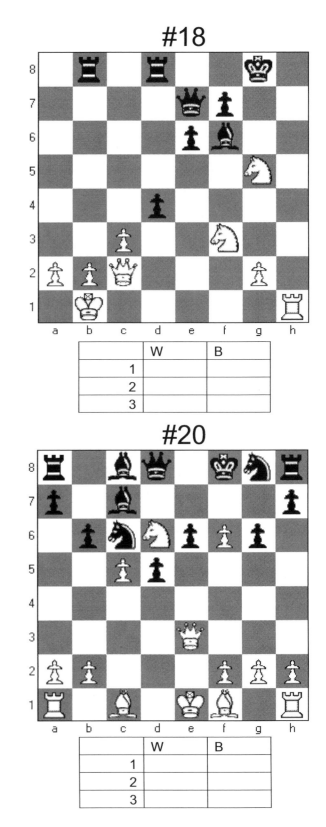

	W	B
1		
2		
3		

#19

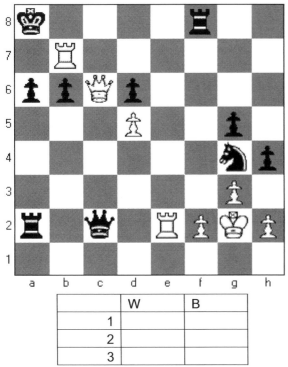

	W	B
1		
2		
3		

#20

	W	B
1		
2		
3		

Mate in 3-First Move Is Not Check

Use chess notation to show how White can checkmate in three moves

#21

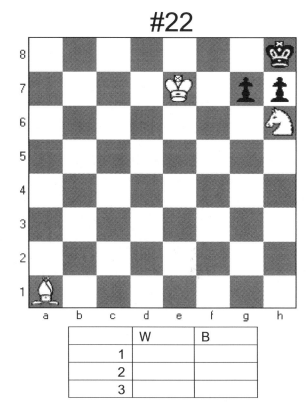

	W	B
1		
2		
3		

#22

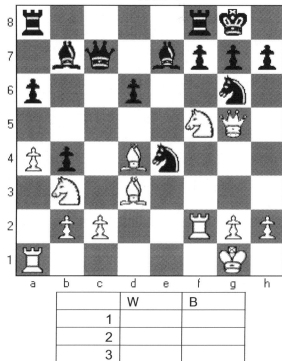

	W	B
1		
2		
3		

#23

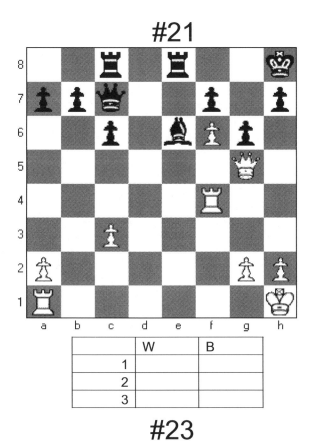

	W	B
1		
2		
3		

#24

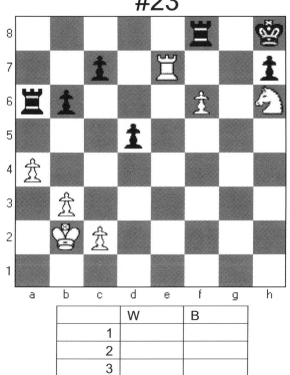

	W	B
1		
2		
3		

Mate in 3-First Move Is Not Check

Use chess notation to show how White can checkmate in three moves

#25

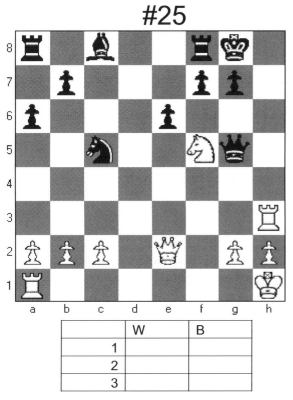

	W	B
1		
2		
3		

#26

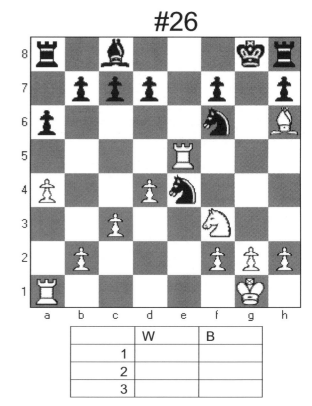

	W	B
1		
2		
3		

#27

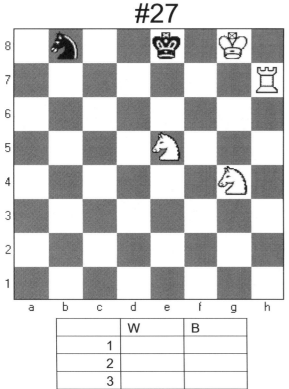

	W	B
1		
2		
3		

#28

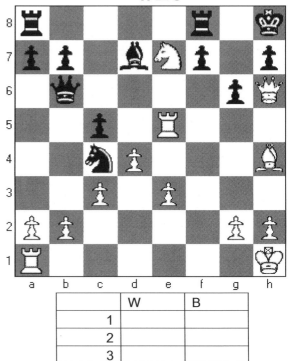

	W	B
1		
2		
3		

Mate in 3-Back Rank

Use chess notation to show how White can checkmate in three moves

#29

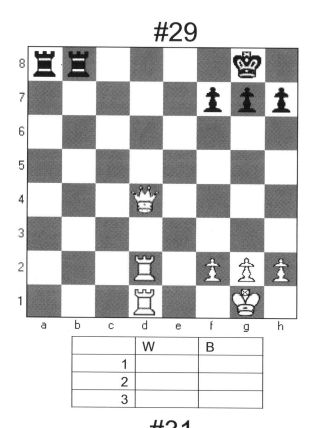

	W	B
1		
2		
3		

#30

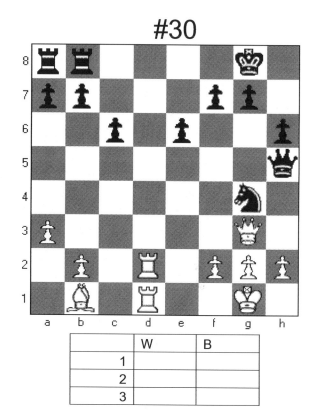

	W	B
1		
2		
3		

#31

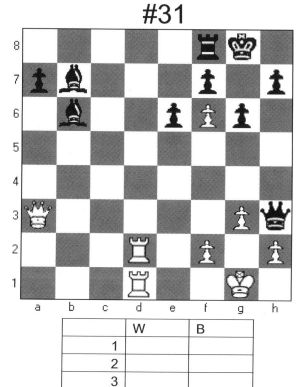

	W	B
1		
2		
3		

#32

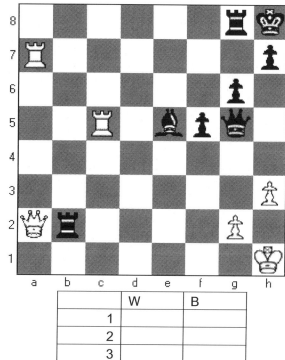

	W	B
1		
2		
3		

Mate in 3-Back Rank

Use chess notation to show how White can checkmate in three moves

#33

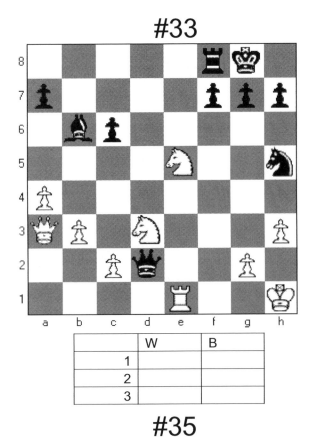

	W	B
1		
2		
3		

#34

	W	B
1		
2		
3		

#35

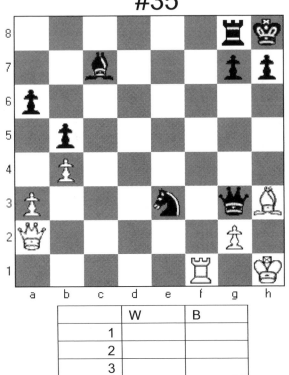

	W	B
1		
2		
3		

#36

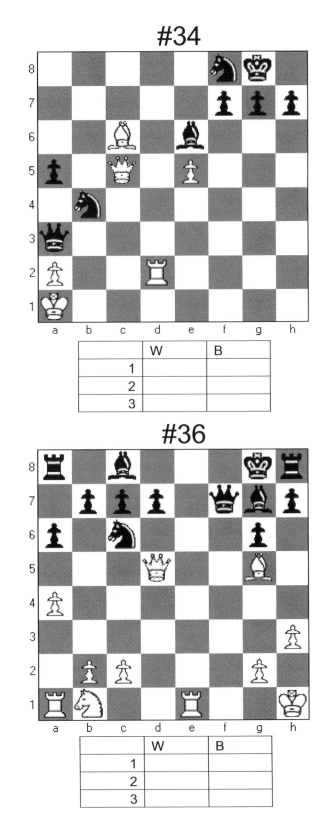

	W	B
1		
2		
3		

Mate in 3-Back Rank

Use chess notation to show how White can checkmate in three moves

#37

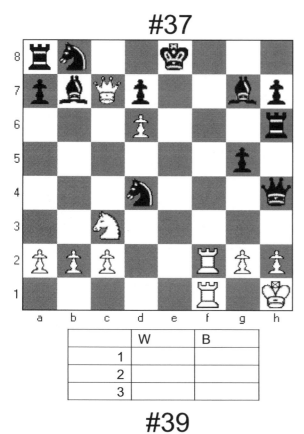

	W	B
1		
2		
3		

#38

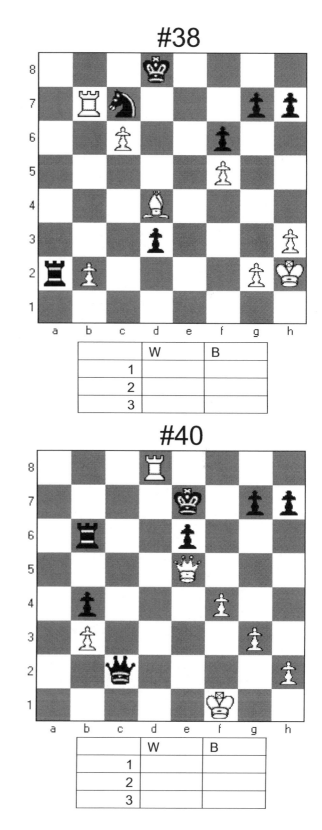

	W	B
1		
2		
3		

#39

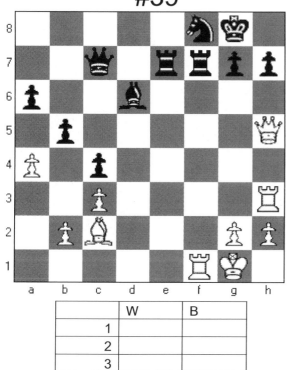

	W	B
1		
2		
3		

#40

	W	B
1		
2		
3		

Mate in 3-Smothered Mate

Use chess notation to show how White can checkmate in three moves

#41

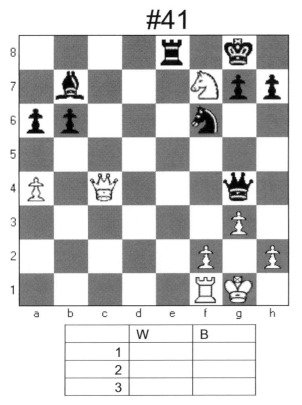

	W	B
1		
2		
3		

#42

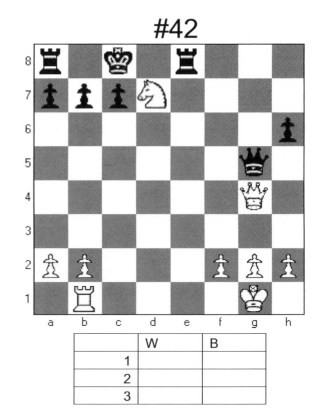

	W	B
1		
2		
3		

#43

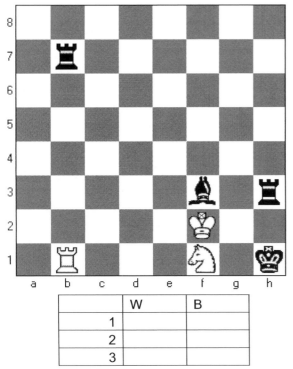

	W	B
1		
2		
3		

#44

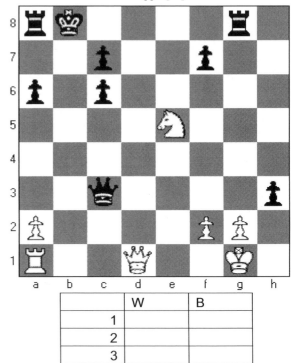

	W	B
1		
2		
3		

Mate in 3-Smothered Mate

Use chess notation to show how White can checkmate in three moves

#45

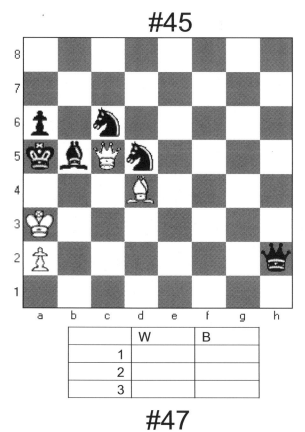

	W	B
1		
2		
3		

#46

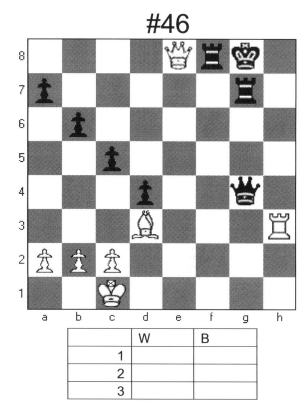

	W	B
1		
2		
3		

#47

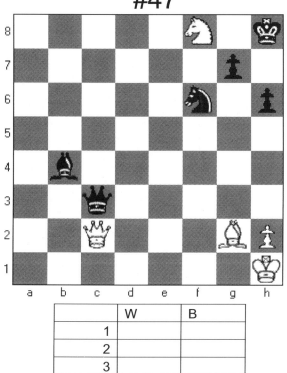

	W	B
1		
2		
3		

#48

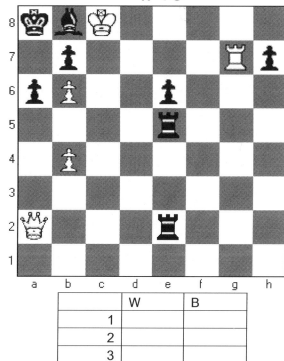

	W	B
1		
2		
3		

Mate in 3-Queen and Helper

Use chess notation to show how White can checkmate in three moves

#49

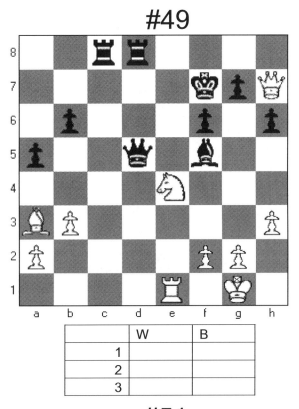

	W	B
1		
2		
3		

#50

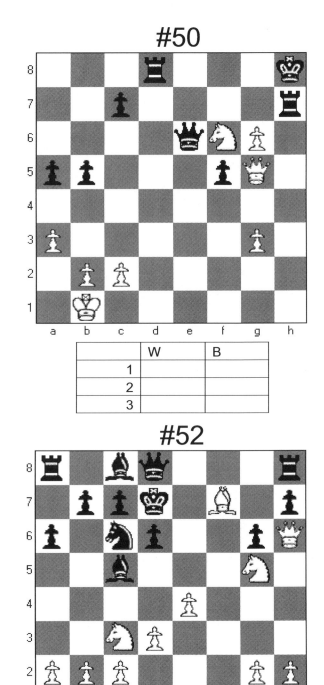

	W	B
1		
2		
3		

#51

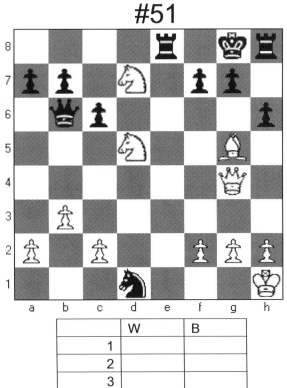

	W	B
1		
2		
3		

#52

	W	B
1		
2		
3		

Mate in 3-Using a Pin

Use chess notation to show how White can checkmate in three moves

#53

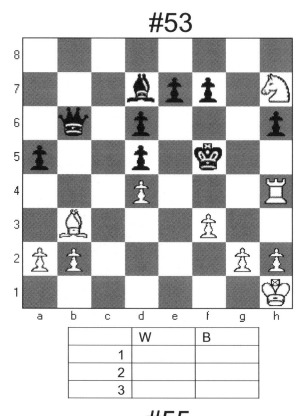

	W	B
1		
2		
3		

#54

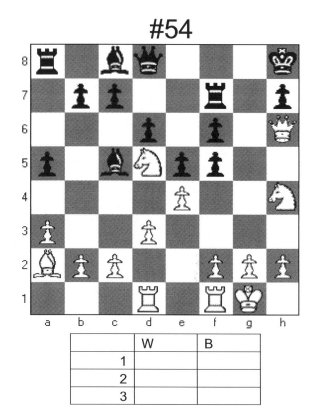

	W	B
1		
2		
3		

#55

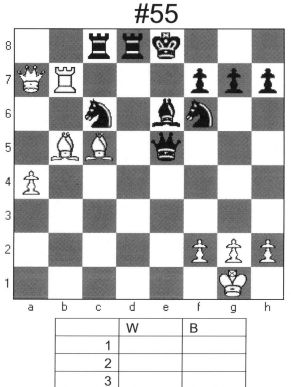

	W	B
1		
2		
3		

#56

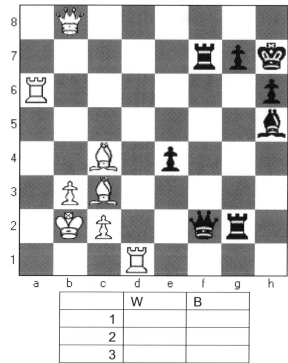

	W	B
1		
2		
3		

Mate in 3-Using a Double Check

Use chess notation to show how White can checkmate in three moves

#57

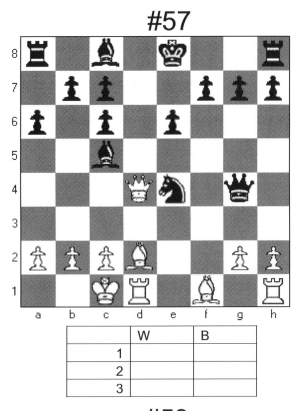

	W	B
1		
2		
3		

#58

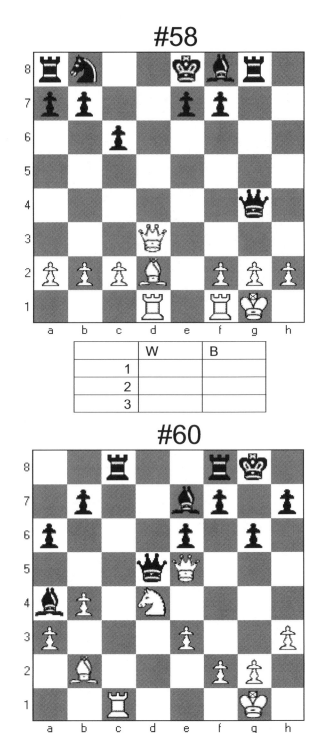

	W	B
1		
2		
3		

#59

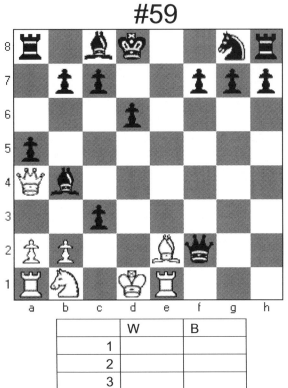

	W	B
1		
2		
3		

#60

	W	B
1		
2		
3		

Mate in 3-Using a Double Check

Use chess notation to show how White can checkmate in three moves

#61

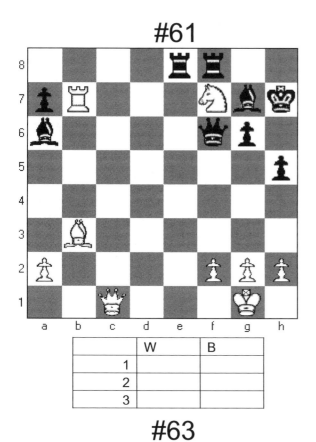

	W	B
1		
2		
3		

#62

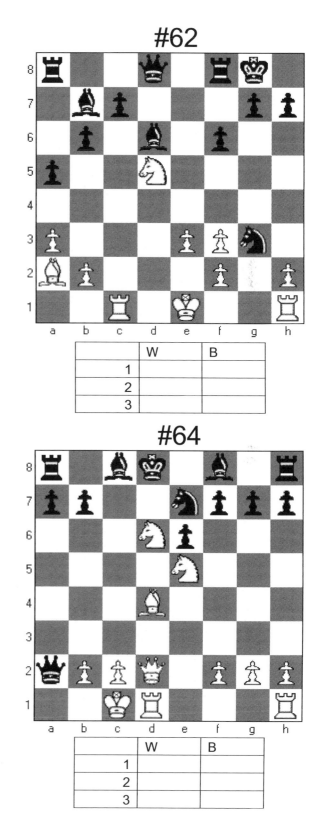

	W	B
1		
2		
3		

#63

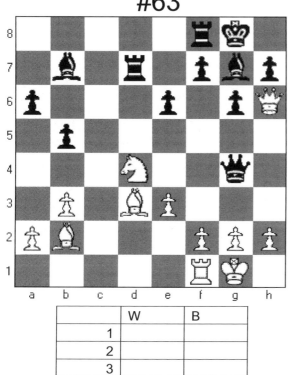

	W	B
1		
2		
3		

#64

	W	B
1		
2		
3		

Mate in 3-Using the h-file

Use chess notation to show how White can checkmate in three moves

#65

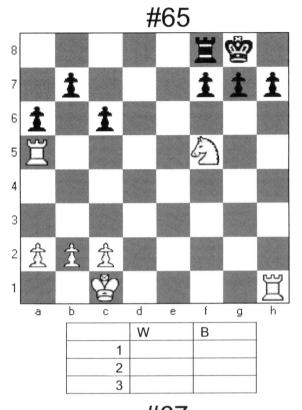

	W	B
1		
2		
3		

#66

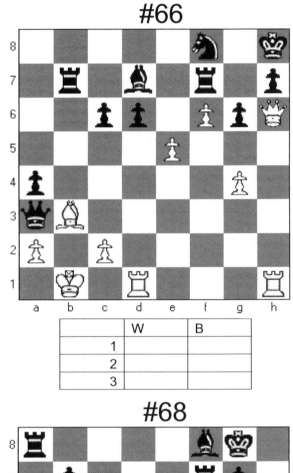

	W	B
1		
2		
3		

#67

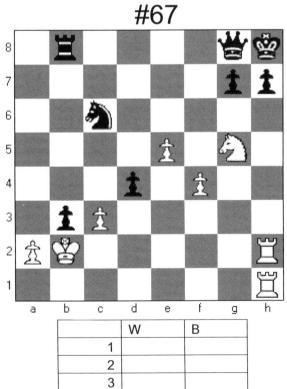

	W	B
1		
2		
3		

#68

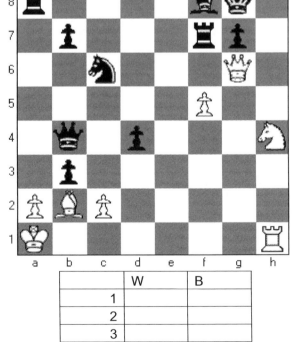

	W	B
1		
2		
3		

Mate in 3-Using the h-file

Use chess notation to show how White can checkmate in three moves

#69

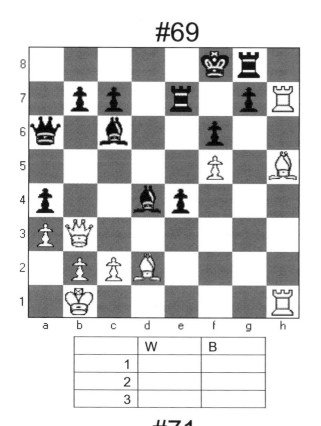

	W	B
1		
2		
3		

#70

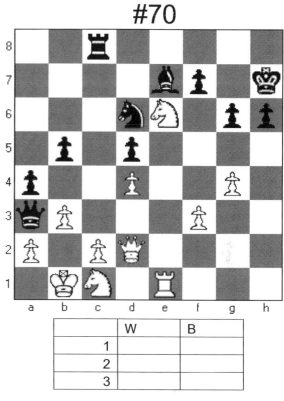

	W	B
1		
2		
3		

#71

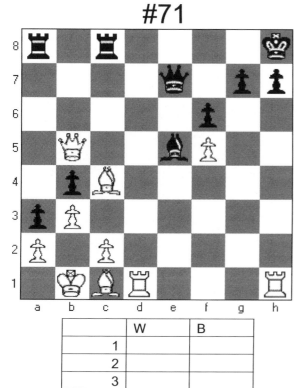

	W	B
1		
2		
3		

#72

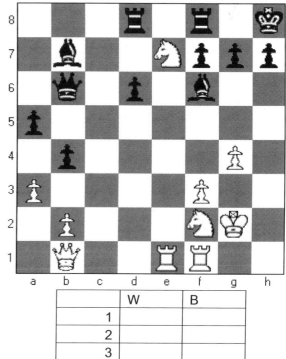

	W	B
1		
2		
3		

Mate in 3-Using the h-file

Use chess notation to show how White can checkmate in three moves

#73

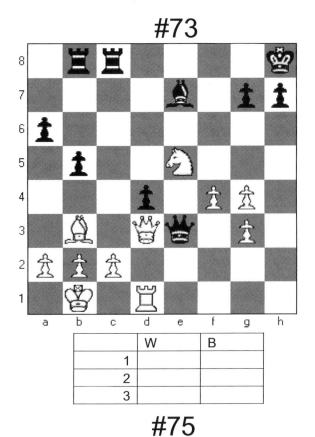

	W	B
1		
2		
3		

#74

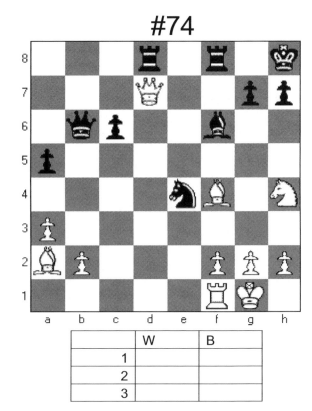

	W	B
1		
2		
3		

#75

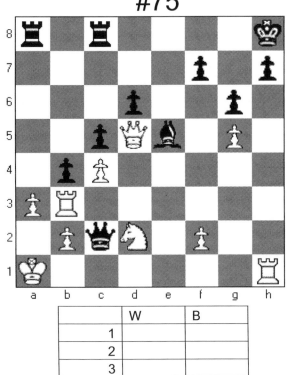

	W	B
1		
2		
3		

#76

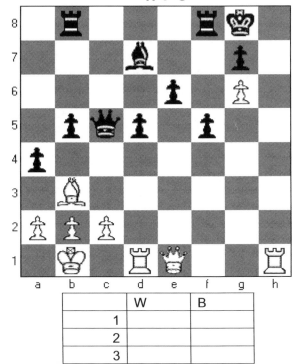

	W	B
1		
2		
3		

Mate in 3-Difficult!

Use chess notation to show how White can checkmate in three moves

#77

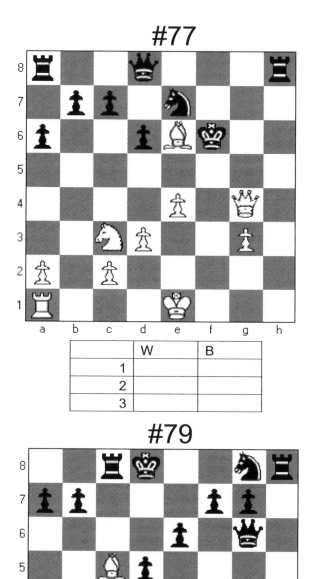

	W	B
1		
2		
3		

#78

	W	B
1		
2		
3		

#79

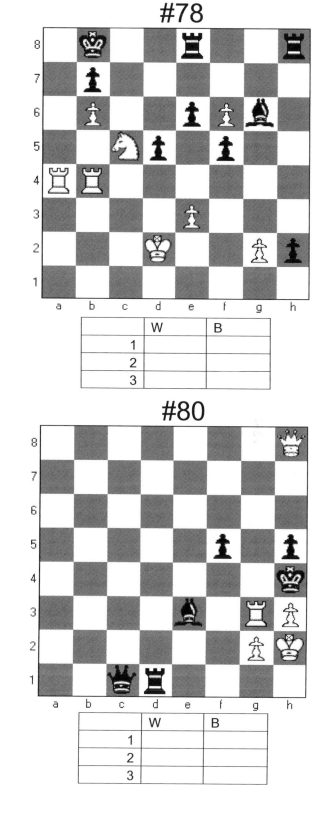

	W	B
1		
2		
3		

#80

	W	B
1		
2		
3		

Mate in 3-Difficult!

Use chess notation to show how White can checkmate in three moves

#81

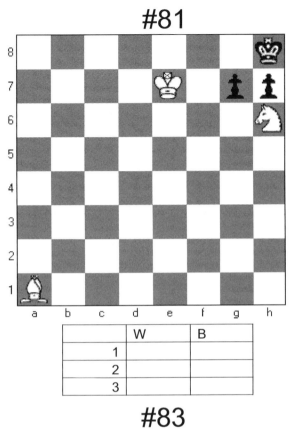

	W	B
1		
2		
3		

#82

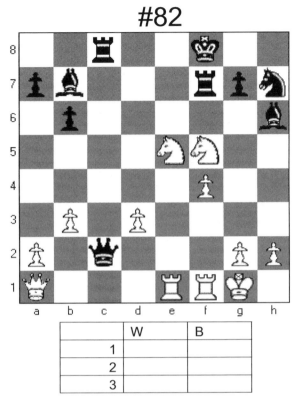

	W	B
1		
2		
3		

#83

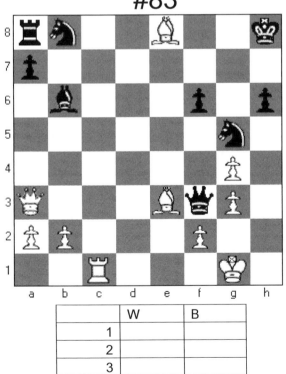

	W	B
1		
2		
3		

#84

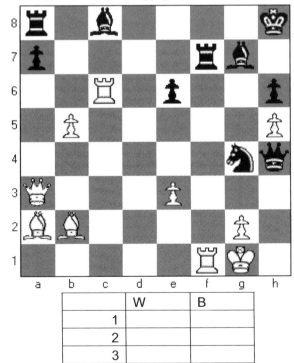

	W	B
1		
2		
3		

Mate in 3-Difficult!

Use chess notation to show how White can checkmate in three moves

#85

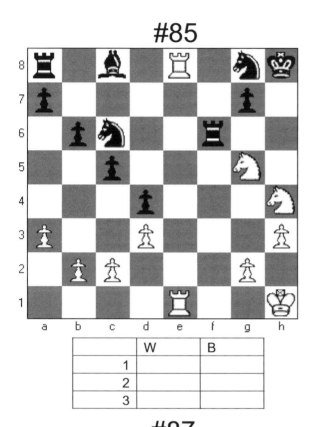

	W	B
1		
2		
3		

#86

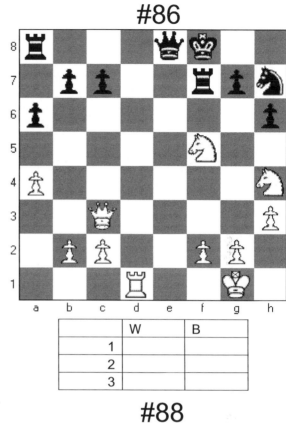

	W	B
1		
2		
3		

#87

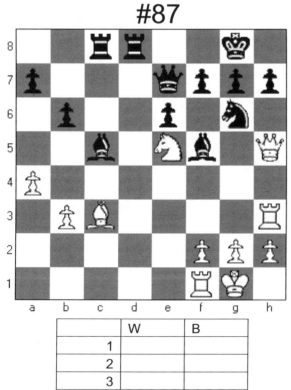

	W	B
1		
2		
3		

#88

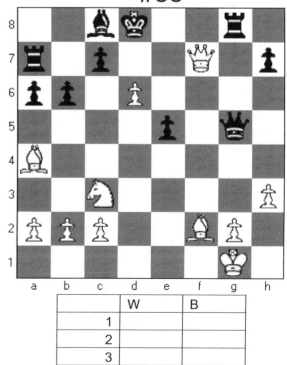

	W	B
1		
2		
3		

Mate in 3-Difficult!

Use chess notation to show how White can checkmate in three moves

#89

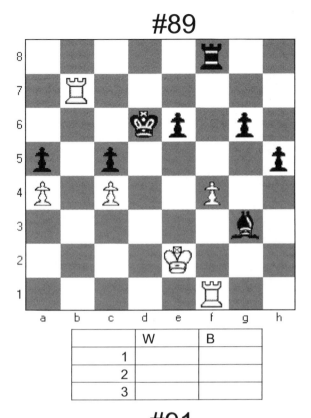

	W	B
1		
2		
3		

#90

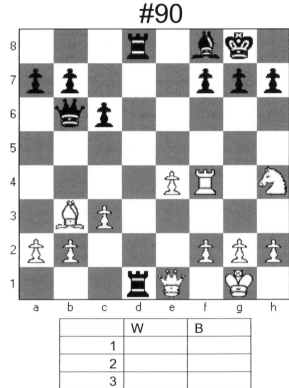

	W	B
1		
2		
3		

#91

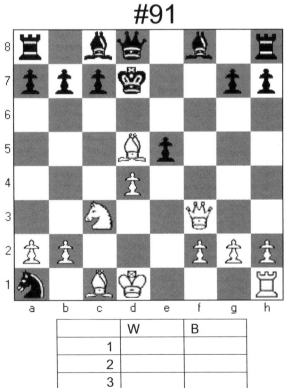

	W	B
1		
2		
3		

#92

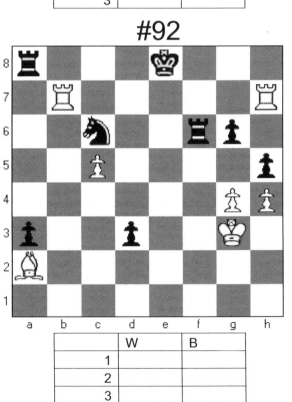

	W	B
1		
2		
3		

Mate in 3-Difficult!

Use chess notation to show how White can checkmate in three moves

#93

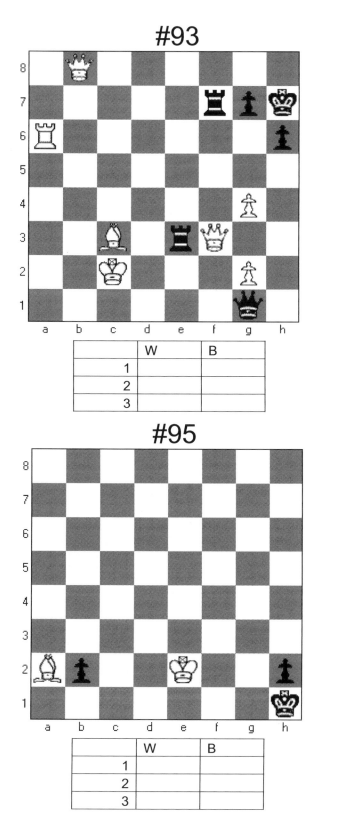

	W	B
1		
2		
3		

#94

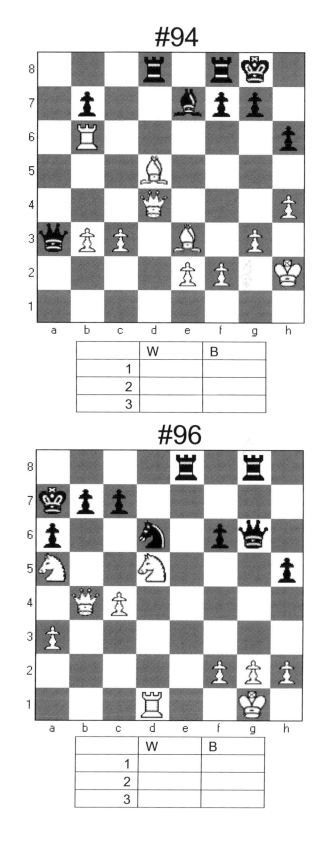

	W	B
1		
2		
3		

#95

	W	B
1		
2		
3		

#96

	W	B
1		
2		
3		

Mate in 3-Difficult!

Use chess notation to show how White can checkmate in three moves

#97

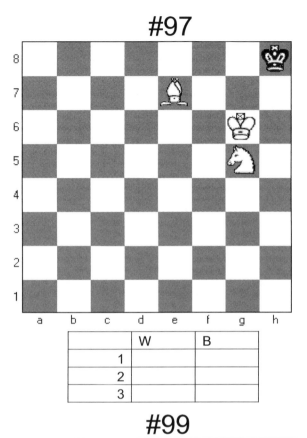

	W	B
1		
2		
3		

#98

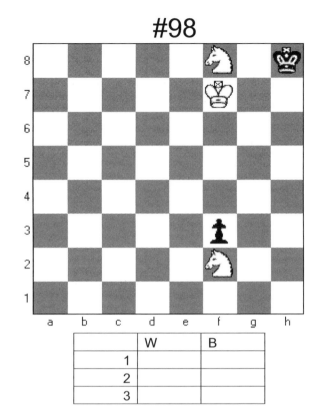

	W	B
1		
2		
3		

#99

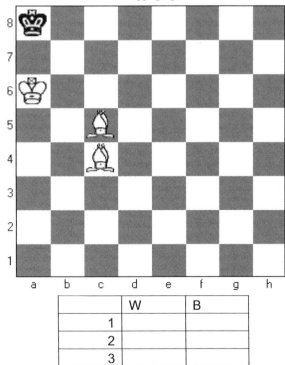

	W	B
1		
2		
3		

#100

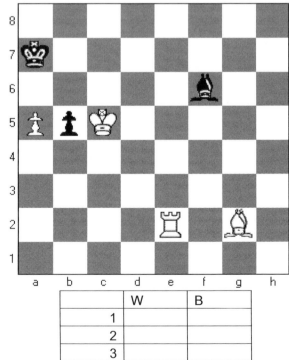

	W	B
1		
2		
3		

Chapter 5-Checkmate in 4 Moves

This is a short chapter. By now, you have experience with more difficult problems. This section is designed more as a test. There may be more than 1 alternative move for Black here. You must give all the variations. So for instance, if he has 2 choices and one leads to mate in 2 and another to mate in 4, you must give BOTH. Try to complete all 8 mate in 4 problems successfully in less than 30 minutes. Our master can solve all 8 in 15 minutes.

Good luck!

Mate in 4

Use chess notation to show how White can checkmate in four moves

#1

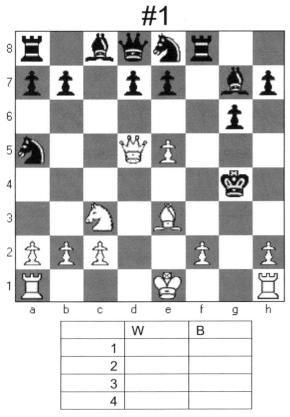

	W	B
1		
2		
3		
4		

#2

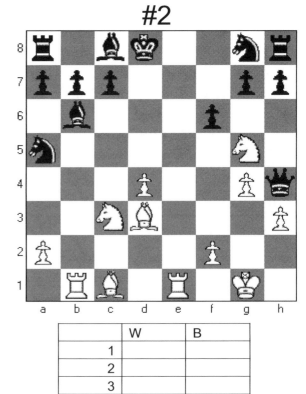

	W	B
1		
2		
3		
4		

#3

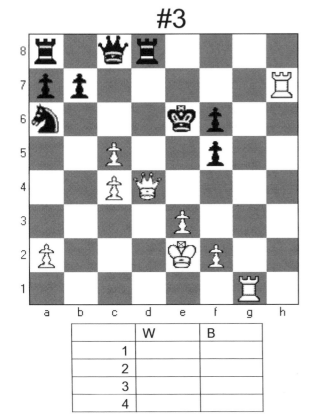

	W	B
1		
2		
3		
4		

#4

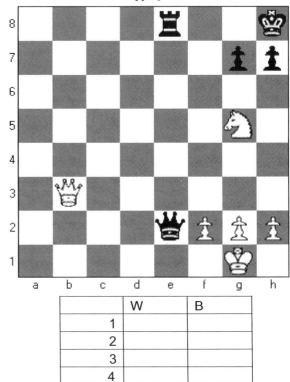

	W	B
1		
2		
3		
4		

Mate in 4

Use chess notation to show how White can checkmate in four moves

#5

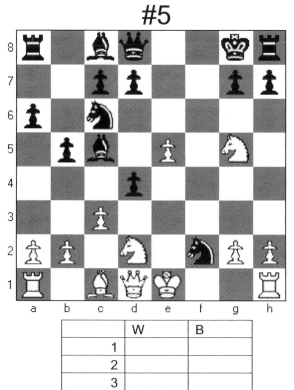

	W	B
1		
2		
3		
4		

#6

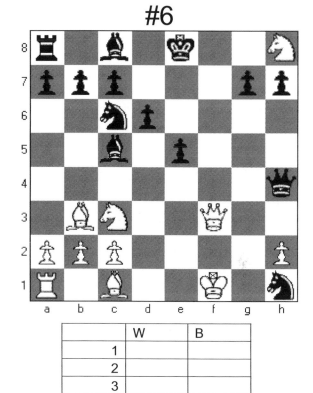

	W	B
1		
2		
3		
4		

#7

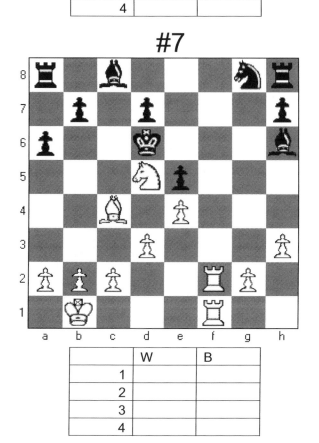

	W	B
1		
2		
3		
4		

#8

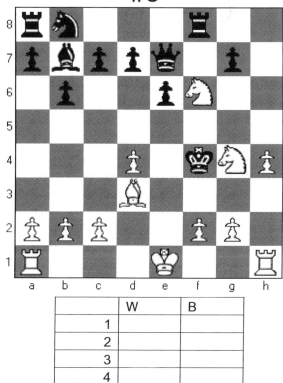

	W	B
1		
2		
3		
4		

Chapter 6-Legall's Checkmate

One of the most useful types of specialty checkmate patterns is the so-called 'Legall's Checkmate'. It was named after the French chessplayer Legall De Kermeur who lived from 1702-1792. He was one of the best, if not the best chess player in his day until his student Francois-Andre Danican Philidor surpassed him. Legall had his name attached to the checkmate after a famous queen sacrifice game he played in 1750.

Let's take a look at a key position using this Legall's checkmate idea:

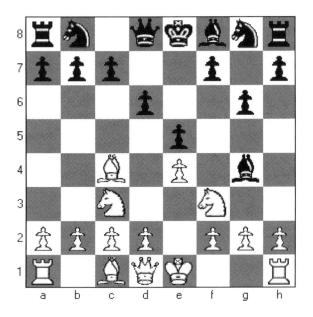

Black's bishop pins White's knight to White's queen. Pins are annoying, and there are 4 main ways to deal with them:

1-the kick (P-h3 would be an example of the kick; White wants to kick the bishop out of there)

2-the block (B-e2 would be an example of the block. The bishop comes back to block Black's bishops pin, effectively breaking the pin and freeing up White's knight to move)

3-the run (Q-e2 and then Q-e3 runs the queen out of the way of the pin freeing up the knight to move)

4-the challenge! See below

Three of the four main ways of dealing with a pin are aimed at eliminating the power of the pin. If you had to deal with a pin 100 times, you would use the first three ways 99 out of the 100 times.

The challenge is the way to deal with a pin that works only one in 100 times. In the above position, White can use the challenge which basically says 'I don't care if my knight is pinned, I'm moving him anyway!!'

Chapter 6-Legall's Checkmates

Here's how White can win material or the game using Legall's checkmate.

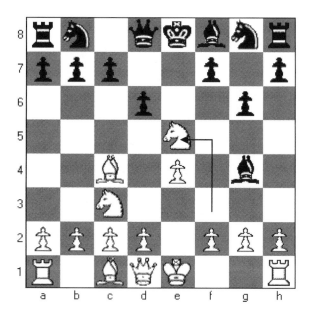

Nxe5!

White captures the pawn on e5 exposing his queen to Black's bishop.

Black can capture the knight with Pxe5, but then White would play Qxg4 and win Black's bishop.

So what do you think Black did?

Of course, he took the queen!!

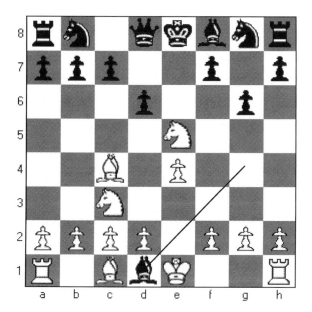

Now White can force checkmate in 2 moves.

Q: Can you find it?

Chapter 6-Legall's Checkmates

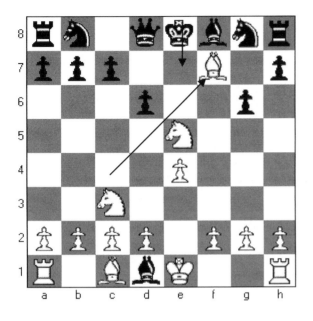

A: Bxf7+

White's bishop attacks Black's king. The bishop is defended by his knight on e5. The Black king has only one move. He must go to e7.

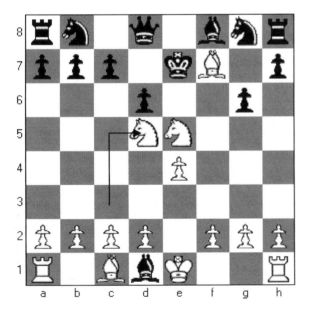

Then N-d5 is checkmate.

The king is under attack from one knight. White's other knight and bishop take away Black's other squares. And finally, Black's queen, bishop on f8 and pawn on d6 prevent him from running away.

So that is Legall's checkmate!

Remember this advanced pattern as we move on to Legall's checkmate problems!

Our master can solve all of these in 5 minutes!

Legall's Checkmate Problems-Mate in 1

Draw an arrow or use chess notation to show how White can checkmate in one move

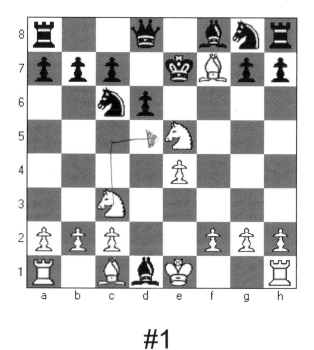

#1

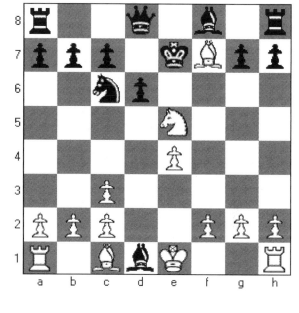

#2

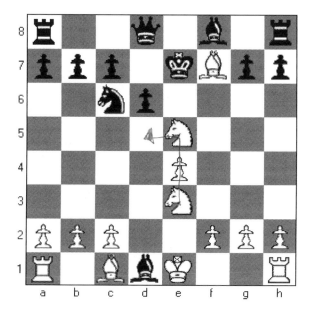

#3

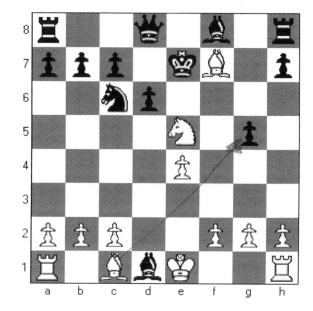

#4

Legall's Checkmate Problems-Mate in 2

Draw arrows or use chess notation to show how White can checkmate in two moves

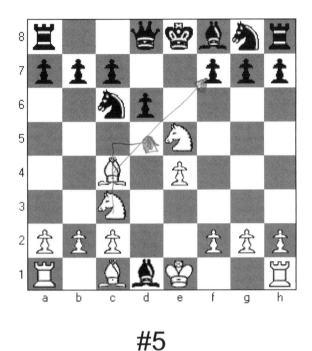

#5

#6

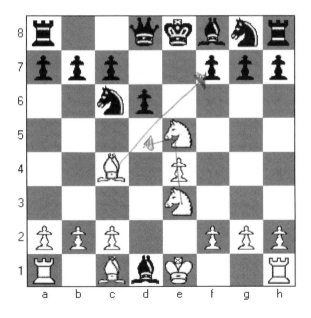

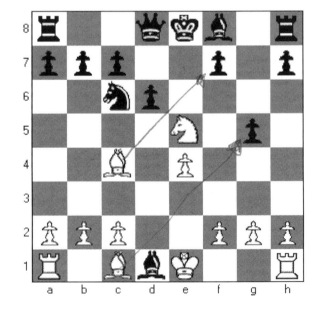

#7

#8

Legall's Checkmate Problems-Difficult!

Draw arrows or use chess notation to show White's best move (White must win material, even if it is just a pawn!)

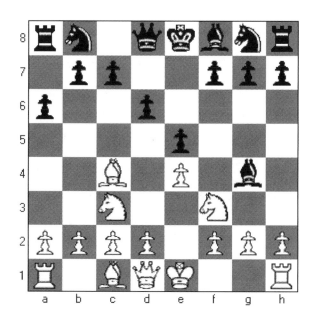

#9

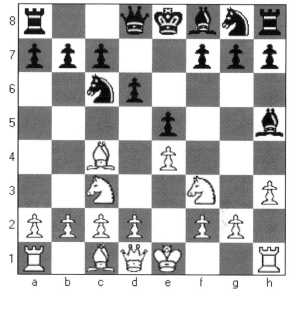

#10

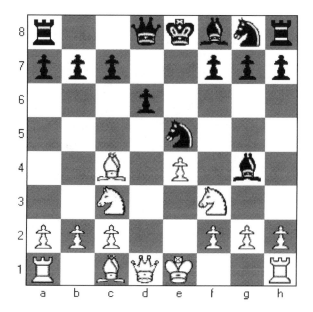

#11

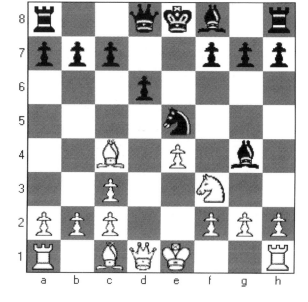

#12

Chapter 7-Triple Loyd's

Sam Loyd was a great American creator of chess puzzles. He created positions in which there would be three separate things to accomplish.

You'll notice that there is no Black king on the board in these problems. Your job is to place the Black king on a square where it is in checkmate by writing the letter K.

In addition, you will need to find where the king will be in stalemate. Write the letter K and draw a square around it.

Finally, you will need to find where you will be able to make one move to checkmate the Black king. Write in the letter K and draw a circle around it.

As you might imagine, it is usually easiest to find the square where the king is in checkmate.

One last tip is that the square where the king can be stalemated and where it can be checkmated in 1 move MAY be the same square.

Our master can solve this entire section in 15 minutes.

Good luck!

Triple Loyd's

In each of the diagrams, place the Black king on the board to make checkmate, stalemate, and mate in one. Use these symbols:

K = checkmate | K | = stalemate   (K) = mate in one

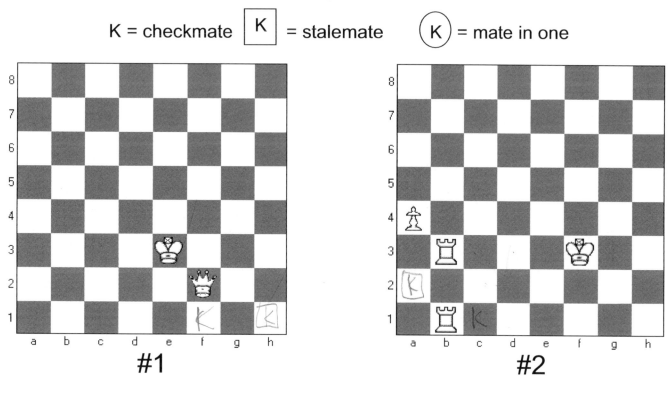

#1

#2

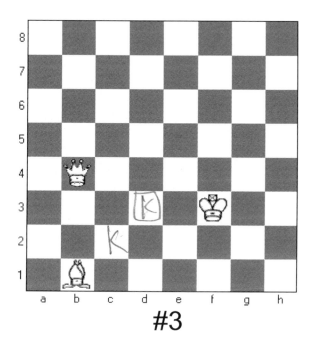

#3

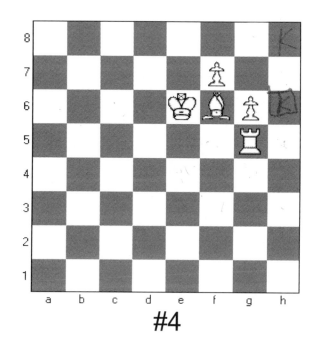

#4

Triple Loyd's

In each of the diagrams, place the Black king on the board to make checkmate, stalemate, and mate in one. Use these symbols:

K = checkmate $\boxed{K}$ = stalemate $\binom{K}$ = mate in one

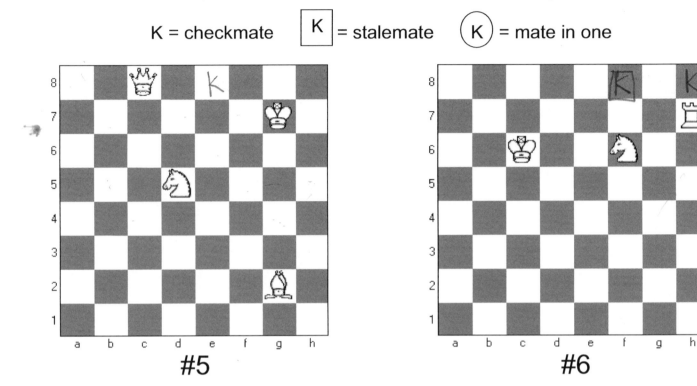

#5

#6

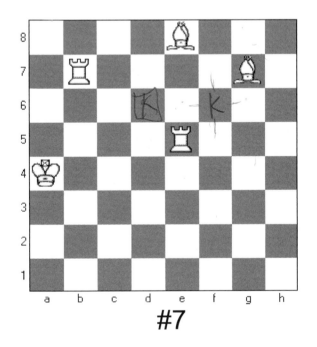

#7

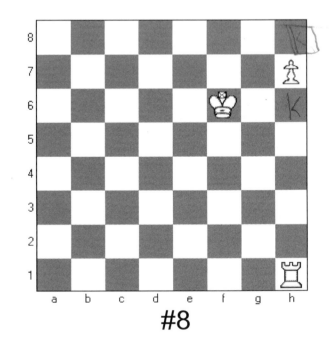

#8

Chapter 8-Frame by Frames

Frame by Frames is a technique designed for pattern recognition. In this technique the first frame you see, you will solve for mate in 1 move. The second frame that you see, will be the move just prior to the mate in 1 move, which is mate in 2 moves. This pattern repeats through frames 3 and 4.

Try the first few problems in order, finding the mate in 1 first then mate in 2 then 3, then 4.

Once you get the hang of it challenge yourself by trying to figure out the mate in 3 or 4 without doing the mate in 1 and 2 first.

Our master can solve all 4 problems on each page in less than 1 minute!

Good luck!

Frame by Frame #1-Smothered Mate

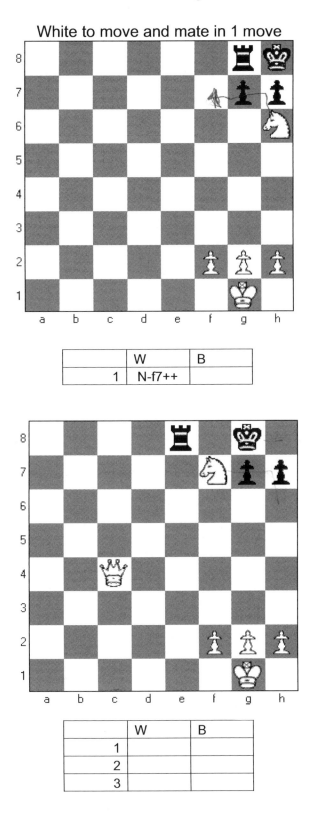

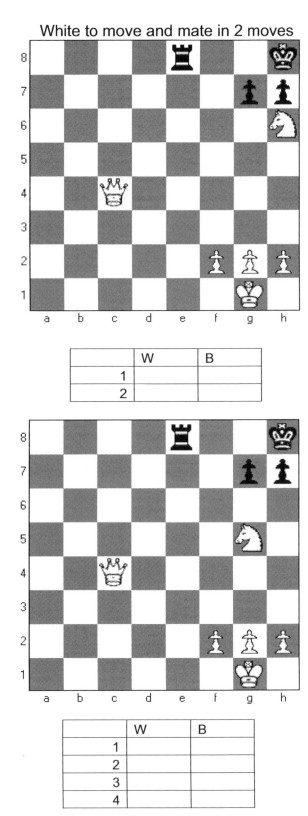

White to move and mate in 1 move

	W	B
1	N-f7++	

White to move and mate in 2 moves

	W	B
1		
2		

	W	B
1		
2		
3		

	W	B
1		
2		
3		
4		

White to move and mate in 3 moves

White to move and mate in 4 moves

Frame by Frame #2-King Run

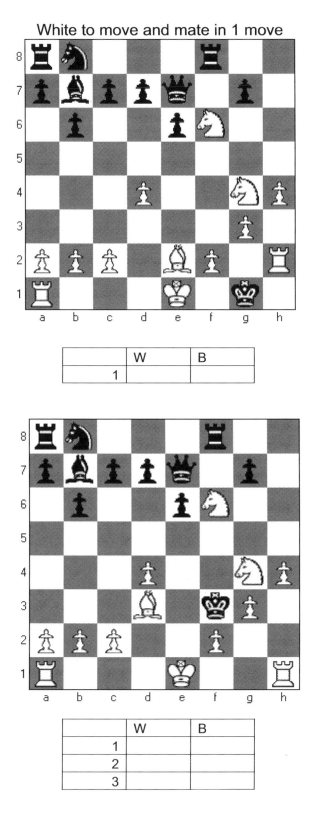

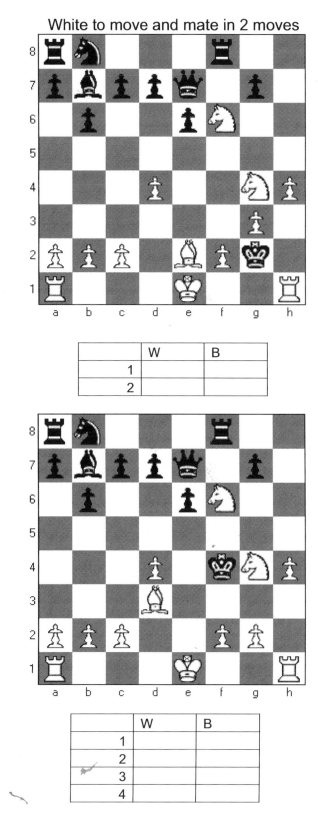

White to move and mate in 1 move

	W	B
1		

White to move and mate in 2 moves

	W	B
1		
2		

White to move and mate in 3 moves

	W	B
1		
2		
3		

White to move and mate in 4 moves

	W	B
1		
2		
3		
4		

Frame by Frame #3-h-file

White to move and mate in 1 move

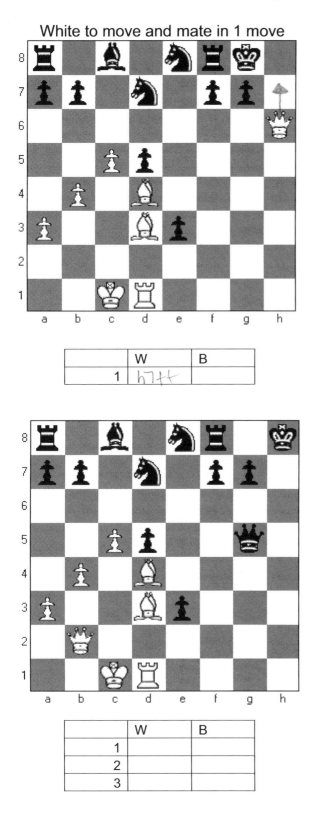

	W	B
1	h7++	

White to move and mate in 2 moves

	W	B
1		
2		

White to move and mate in 3 moves

	W	B
1		
2		
3		

White to move and mate in 4 moves

	W	B
1		
2		
3		
4		

Frame by Frame #4-h-file

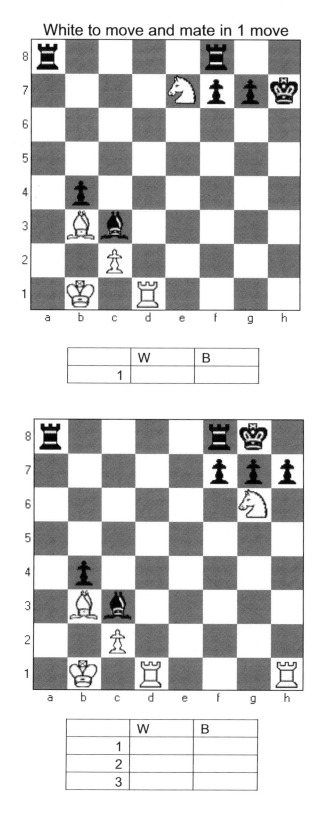

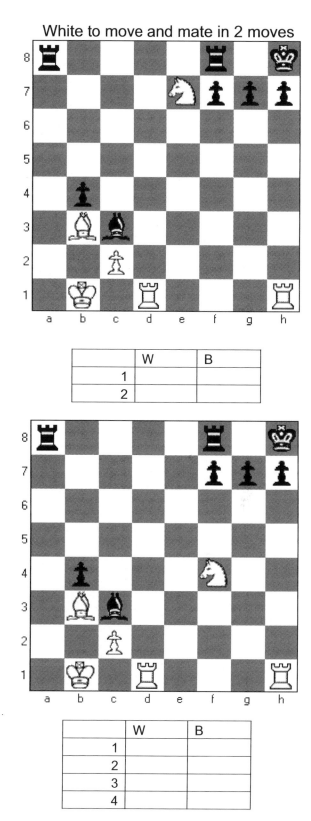

White to move and mate in 1 move

	W	B
1		

White to move and mate in 2 moves

	W	B
1		
2		

	W	B
1		
2		
3		

	W	B
1		
2		
3		
4		

White to move and mate in 3 moves

White to move and mate in 4 moves

Frame by Frame #5-Back Rank

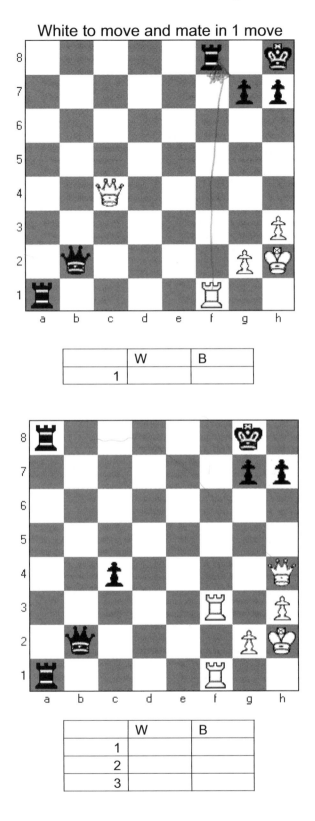

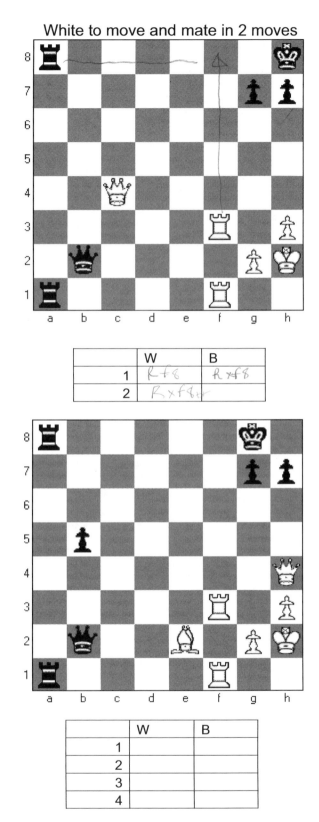

White to move and mate in 1 move

	W	B
1		

White to move and mate in 2 moves

	W	B
1	Rf8	Rxf8
2	Rxf8#	

White to move and mate in 3 moves

	W	B
1		
2		
3		

White to move and mate in 4 moves

	W	B
1		
2		
3		
4		

Frame by Frame #6-Back Rank

Black to move and mate in 1 move

Black to move and mate in 2 moves

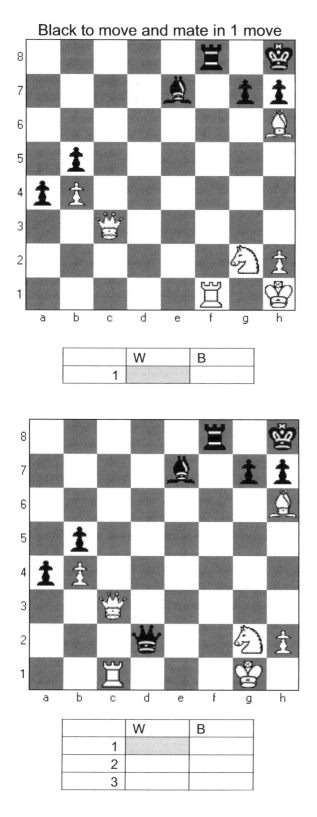

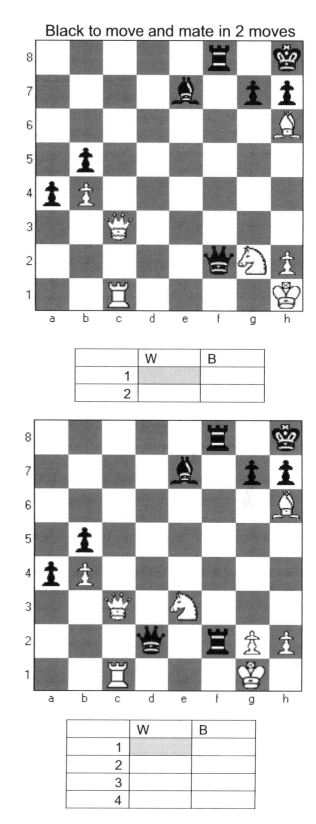

	W	B
1		

	W	B
1		
2		

	W	B
1		
2		
3		

	W	B
1		
2		
3		
4		

Black to move and mate in 3 moves

Black to move and mate in 4 moves

Frame by Frame #7-Queen and Helper

White to move and mate in 1 move

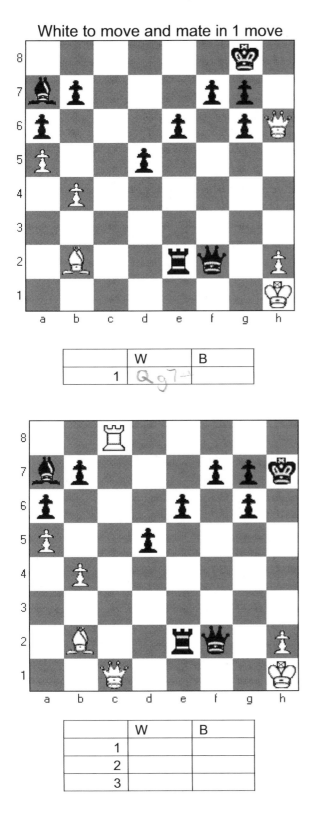

	W	B
1	Qg7~	

White to move and mate in 2 moves

	W	B
1		
2		

White to move and mate in 3 moves

	W	B
1		
2		
3		

White to move and mate in 4 moves

	W	B
1		
2		
3		
4		

Frame by Frame #8-Queen and Helper

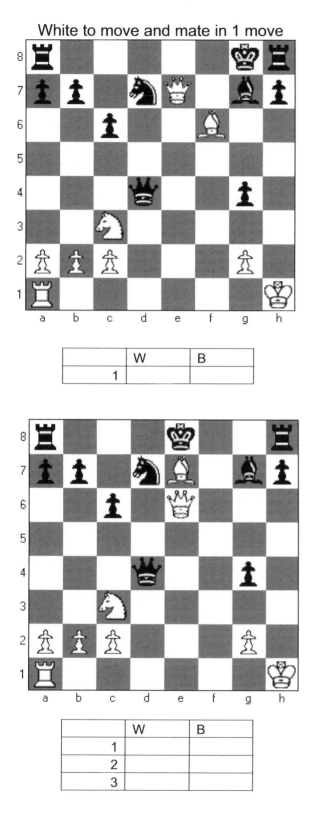

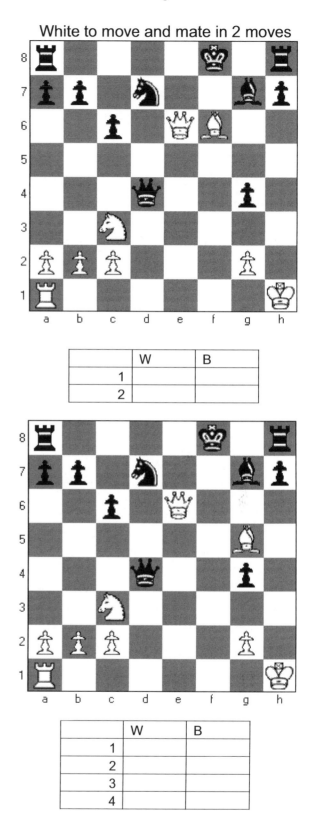

White to move and mate in 1 move

	W	B
1		

White to move and mate in 2 moves

	W	B
1		
2		

	W	B
1		
2		
3		

	W	B
1		
2		
3		
4		

White to move and mate in 3 moves

White to move and mate in 4 moves

Frame by Frame #9-Remove the Guard

White to move and mate in 1 move

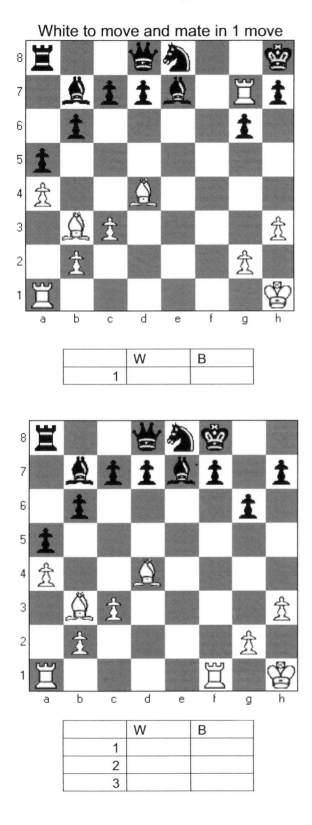

	W	B
1		

White to move and mate in 2 moves

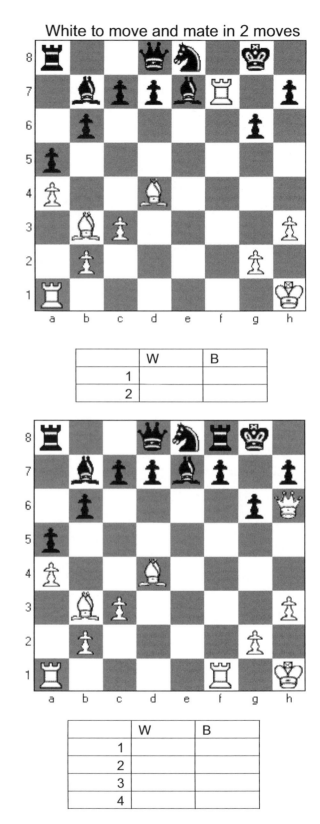

	W	B
1		
2		

	W	B
1		
2		
3		

White to move and mate in 3 moves

	W	B
1		
2		
3		
4		

White to move and mate in 4 moves

Frame by Frame #10-Morphy's Mates

Black to move and mate in 1 move

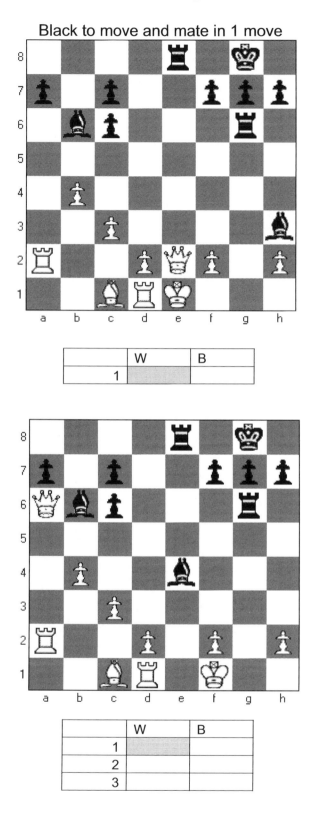

	W	B
1		

Black to move and mate in 2 moves

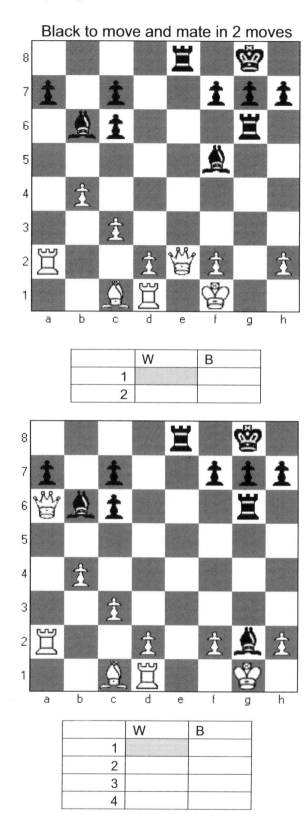

	W	B
1		
2		

	W	B
1		
2		
3		

Black to move and mate in 3 moves

	W	B
1		
2		
3		
4		

Black to move and mate in 4 moves

Chapter 9- Endgames-From Easy to Hard

An endgame is the end of a game. Many chess games end in the opening or middlegame, but some also go on through the endgame. This means that there are not many pieces left on the board. Most have been captured in the opening or middlegame. In this chapter, we are going to be taking a look at some of the most common and most important types of endgames.

2 Rooks and King vs. King

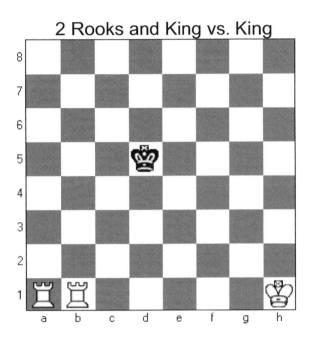

Queen and King vs. King

Rook and King vs. King

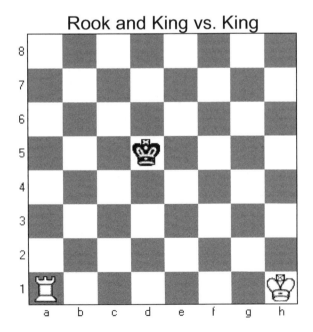

King and Pawn Endgames

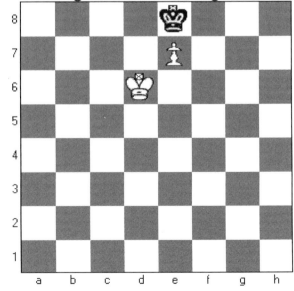

Endgames

Many times an endgame will be reached when your opponent will have only his king left. Do you think it will be easier to checkmate his king if it is in the middle of the chessboard or on the side of the chessboard?

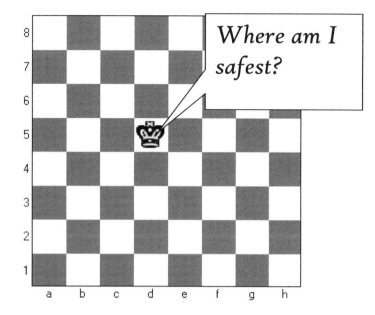

If the king is the only piece left, it will be safest **in the middle of the chessboard.** Can you count the number of squares around the king in the middle of the chessboard?

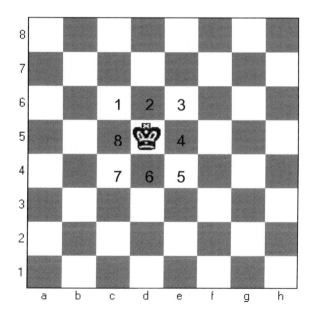

The king can move to 8 different squares from the middle of the chessboard.

Endgames

If the king is on the side of the board it can go to 5 different squares. If the king is in the corner it can go to 3 different squares.

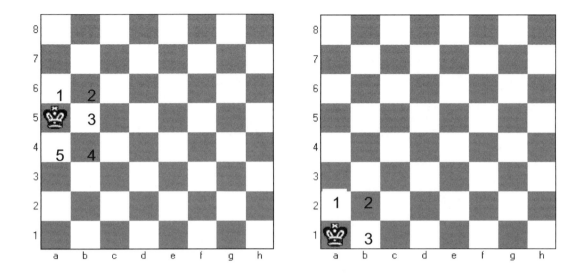

Therefore, the king is safest as he gets closer to the middle of the chessboard. This is the exact opposite of where the king is safest in the opening and middlegame. In the opening and middlegame, we want our king closer to the side of the board. With no helper pieces to protect our king, he is safest in middle because he has more places to run.

Now that we have learned that, it will be easier to figure out how to make checkmates against a lone king. First, we will look at an endgame where two rooks can checkmate a king.

Endgames

Let us start with the following position. Notice how Black's king is on a safer square because he is closer to the middle of the chessboard.

2 Rooks and King vs. King

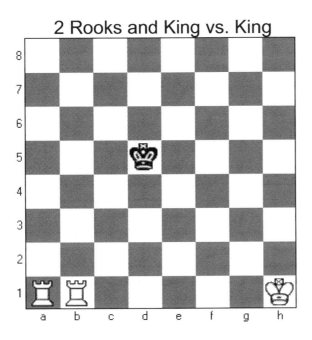

We know that we want to get the Black king toward a side of the chess board. Before we can figure out how to make checkmate, we must imagine how it can happen. In the below diagram, make a checkmate by writing two R's on squares where you would like the White rooks to be:

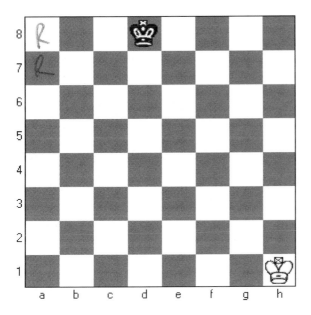

Endgames

Did you find a way to make checkmate?   Let's look at one possible checkmate:

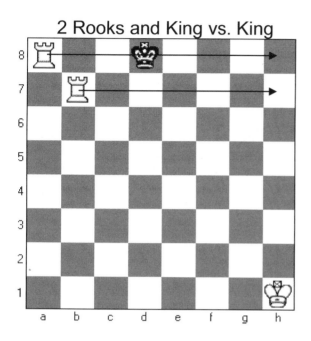

One rook attacks the king from the side, while the other prevents the king from stepping up to the 7th rank.   There are many other possible ways to make a checkmate with 2 rooks against a king.   Now, let us figure out how to get to checkmate!

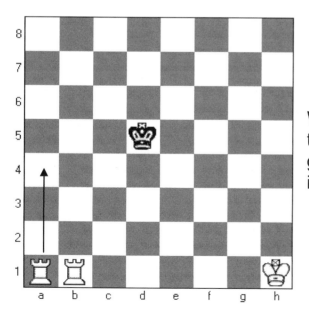

White needs to force the Black king to one of the ends of the chessboard.   Therefore a good first move is Ra4!   Now the Black king is stuck between the 5th to 8th ranks.

Endgames

Our plan is going to be to push the king up the chessboard all the way to the last rank. Our next move will be Rb5+ and the king will have to go back another rank. Our opponent can only try to stop us by bringing the king over.

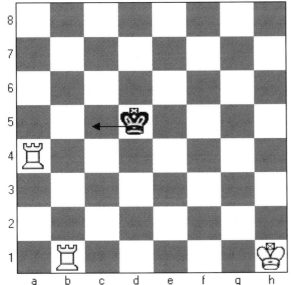

Black can move the king to c5 so that if our rook moves to b5, it will just be captured. It is much harder to checkmate if we only have one rook as we will soon see!

Our rook on b1 needs to find another way to get to the 5th rank. So we can move it all the way to g1, so he stays far away from Black's king.

Black's king can then try to capture our other rook by going to b5. Where should the rook on a4 move to?

Endgames

Our rook should go as far away from the enemy king as possible.

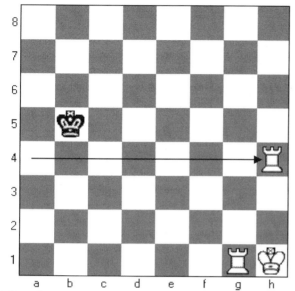

The king can come back to c5, but now we will move our back rook to g5 and check the king back another row.

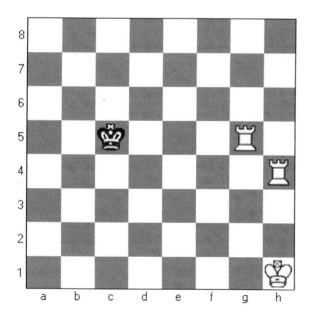

Our plan to get checkmate is going to be to move our rooks like feet. The back foot (rook) goes forward 2 squares until the king gets to the end of the chessboard. We can call this stomping feet! The rooks stomp all of the way to the end of the chessboard.

Endgames

Black's king can do nothing but move toward the White rooks.

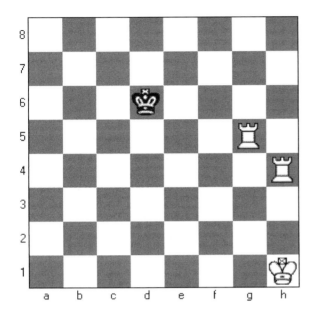

Q: What should White's next move be?

A: Back foot forward! Rh6+

The king can go back to e7. It's time for the back foot to move forward again.

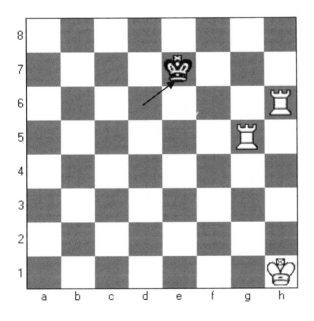

Rg7+ will force the Black king back to the 8th and final rank.

Endgames

Black's king moves toward the White rooks. Rh8 would be checkmate except that he can capture our rook on g7. Can you figure out how White can get checkmate in 2 moves?

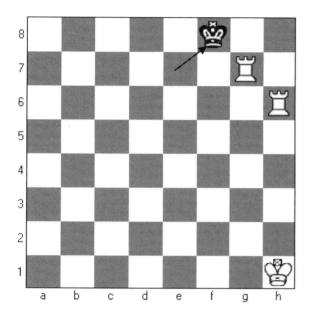

White can protect his attacked rook with the other rook. After Rh7, Black only has one move.

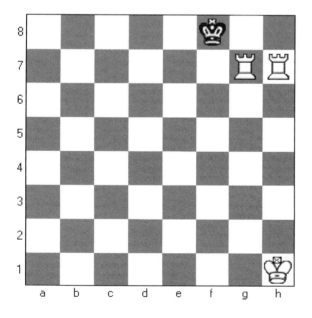

Endgames

Black's king has to move to e8. Now both rooks (feet) are next to each other so either one move forward will win. Rg8 and Rh8 are both checkmate. We forced the Black king all of the way to the end of the chessboard!

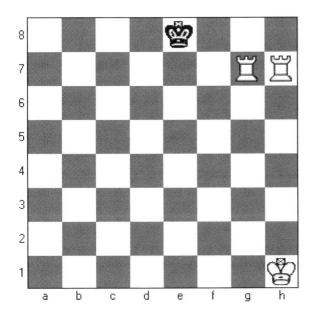

This wasn't too hard was it? You can practice getting checkmate with 2 rooks with a friend. Start out by letting your friend put his or her king in the middle of the chessboard and see how many moves it takes you to get checkmate! Can you make checkmate in less than 10 moves?

Endgames

Now let's move on to one of the most important endgames to be able to win. Queen and king against king endgames happen a lot…and you have to make checkmate in less than 50 moves in tournaments or else the game is declared a draw. If you have the queen, you definitely do not want a draw!

Queen and King vs. King

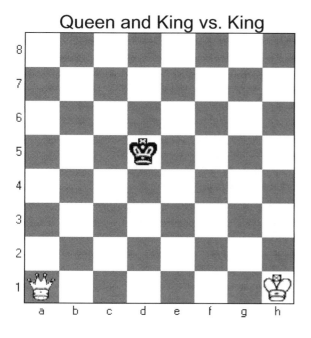

Just like winning with two rooks, we will also need to drive the king to the side of the chessboard. Again, let's try to imagine a position that would be checkmate. In the diagram below, make a checkmate by writing 'Q' on a square where you would like the White queen to be:

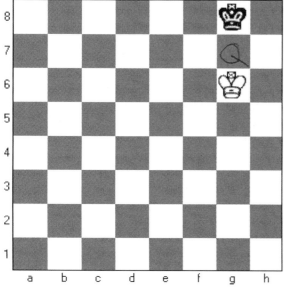

Hint: There are 6 different places to put the White queen to make checkmate.
Challenge: Can you find all six?

Endgames

Did you find any of the checkmates? Let us look at where the Queen could be in order to make a checkmate:

Queen and King vs. King

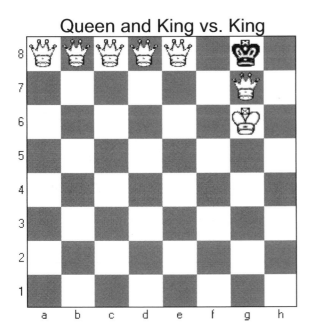

Here are the 6 places you could have placed the queen. Notice how you could have placed the queen to check Black's king from the side on a8, b8, c8, d8, or e8. Checking from f8 would not work because the king would just capture you. That would be a 'Happy Birthday' for your opponent.

The queen could also checkmate on g7. That is because it has a helper piece- your king! Don't forget that king's can be helper's especially in endgames!

Now that we know what we're aiming for, getting there will be easier. We can break down this checkmate into 3 separate steps.

Step 1 is to use your queen only to force the enemy king to the corner of the chessboard. This can be done by moving your queen a knight's move apart from the enemy king until that king can only move back and forth between two squares.

Step 2 is to bring your king toward the enemy king until it is very close (as shown in the diagram above).

Step 3 is to deliver the checkmate by moving your queen to the side or putting your queen next to the enemy king while using your own king as a helper.

Now we're going to see those steps in action!

Endgames

Step one: Using your queen only

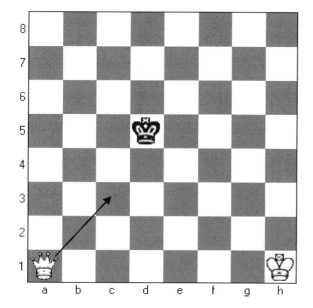

No matter where the enemy king goes we will move the queen a knight's move apart from that king. Our king gets to rest for now.

White starts with Qc3, so that the queen forces the enemy king away from the center. We are going to box in the enemy king.

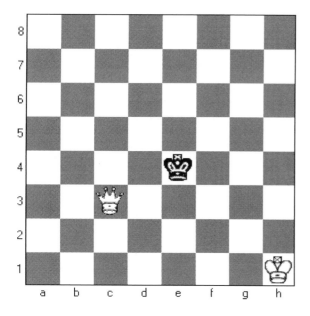

After the Black king moves, where should we move our queen to in order to take away even more squares from the Black king?

Endgames

Step 1: Using your queen only

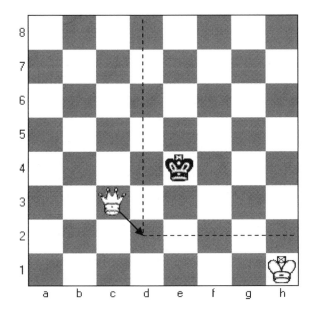

You can move your queen to d2. Now we can see that the enemy king is running out of places to go.

The king is stuck between the dashed lines.

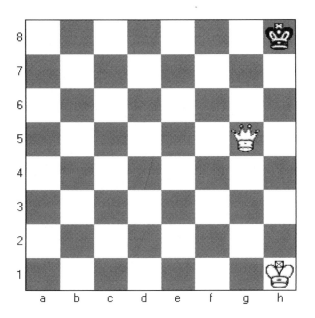

After only a few more moves we will get a position where the enemy king is in the corner of the board. This is when we have to be careful. Should White move the queen to g6 now? Why not?

If the queen goes to g6, the Black king will have no place to go and it will be a stalemate! We have to avoid that!

Step 1 is finished. The queen did a nice job of forcing the king to the edge of the board. Now it's time for the White king to get to work!

Endgames

Step 2: Using your king only

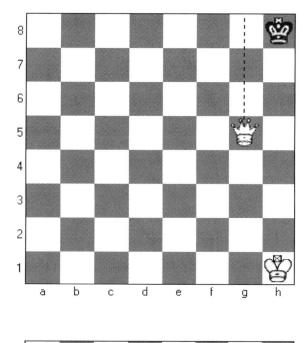

Now our king runs as fast as he can to help the Queen deliver checkmate. The question is, which way does the king go?

If the king runs straight up the board, when he gets to h6, it will be another stalemate!

The king needs to go to the other side. Think of your queen as a bridge and your king and the enemy king should be on opposite sides of the bridge.

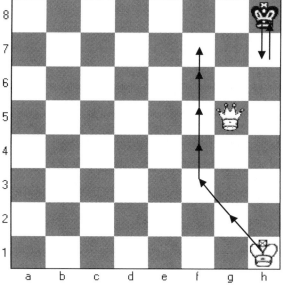

Look at the route that your king can take to stay on the opposite side of the bridge. Meanwhile the Black king can do nothing but shuffle back and forth from h8 to h7.

When the king gets to f6 or f7, step two is complete. The king has successfully finished his journey up the chessboard. Now it is time for the third and final step. This one is the easiest!

Endgames

Step 3: Delivering checkmate

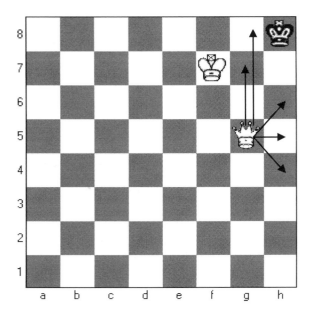

How many ways can you find for White to make checkmate this move?

There are five different moves to make checkmate here.

Three of the checkmates involve the queen checking from the side (h6, h5, h4).

Two of the checkmates have the queen being protected by the White king (g7 and g8).

That's all there is to it! Now practice the starting position against a friend. Try to checkmate in less than 20 moves!

Endgames

Now let's move on to a more challenging endgame. Again, you have to make checkmate in less than 50 moves in tournaments or else the game is declared a draw. If you have the rook, you can make checkmate much faster if you know what to do!

Rook and King vs. King

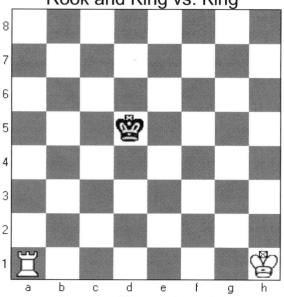

As usual, we will need to drive the king to the side of the chessboard. Again, let's try to imagine a position that would be checkmate. In the diagram below, make a checkmate by writing 'R' on a square where you would like the White rook to be:

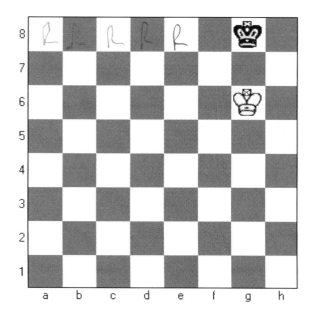

Hint: There are 5 different places to put the White rook to make checkmate.
Challenge: Can you find all five?

Endgames

Did you find any of the checkmates? Let us look at where the rook could be in order to make a checkmate:

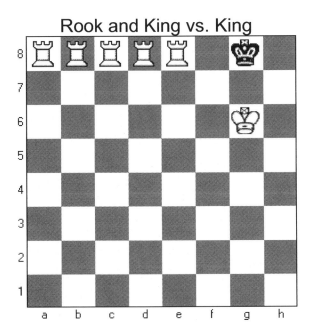

Here are the 5 places you could have placed the rook. Notice how you could have placed the rook to check Black's king from the side on a8, b8, c8, d8, or e8. Checking from f8 or h8 would not work because the king would just capture you.

Now that we know what we're aiming for, getting there will be easier. For this checkmate, we need to remember a pattern.

Step 1 is to use your rook to cut the king off from as much of the board as possible.

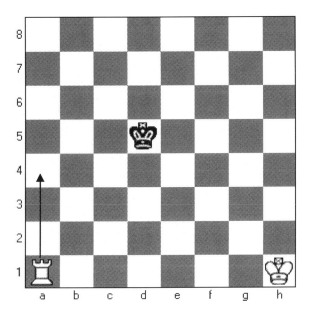

Ra4 is a good first move because the king cannot move past the 5th rank.

Endgames

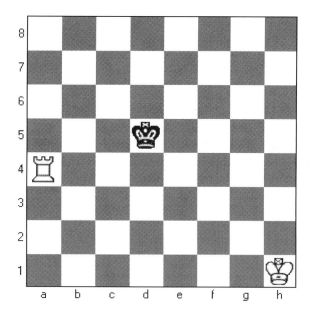

Once our rook prevents his king from advancing, we will need our king's help. Our king needs to help a lot sooner here than when there is a queen.

Our plan is to move our king opposite our opponent's. Right now, we want our king on d3.

Black's king can move around, while our king will head over toward his king. The only time we will move our rook now is if he attacks it or if his king moves backward.

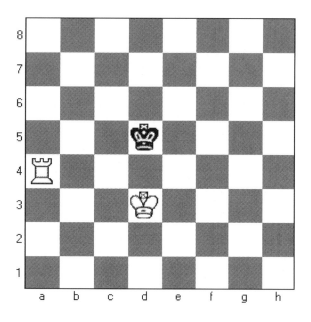

When our kings are opposite each other, it is time to force their king backward. We can do that in this position with ra5. Our king stops his king from moving forward, so he will have to go back to the 6th rank.

Endgames

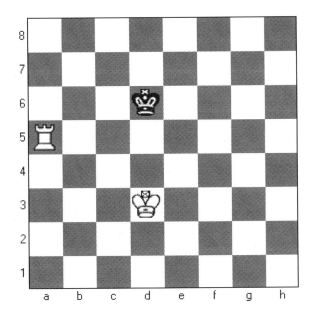

Once his king has moved backward, we will repeat the same idea. We will again make the kings even and then check from the side.

You may be asking, what happens if when we make the kings even, the enemy king moves to the side? Every time we make them even, he will move away as seen below:

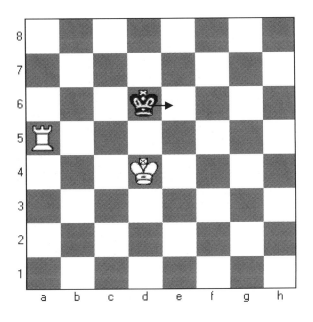

Let us imagine that the Black king moves to e6 here. If our king moves to e4, the enemy king will go back to d6. In this case, we will have to use a trick. We must 'waste a move'. After the Black king goes to e6, we will move our rook to b5. Then it will be Black's turn.

Endgames

Let's jump ahead a few ranks and see how we are going to get checkmate. If it is White's turn here, how would he make checkmate?

Ra8 is checkmate.

Let us now pretend that it is Black's turn. The enemy king wants to run away. How will we make checkmate now?

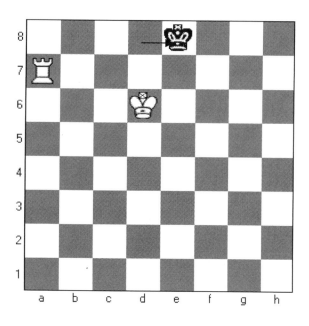

We will have to use the 'waste a move' strategy again. We want to waste a move as far away from his king as possible. This means that b7 is the best place to put our rook. It is far from his king but closer to our king.

Endgames

Now the enemy king can try to run away, but our king will chase him. Eventually, the enemy king will run out of places to go when it hits the end of the board. Then it will be forced to head back toward our king.

After a few moves of chasing the enemy king, it will be forced to come back toward our king.

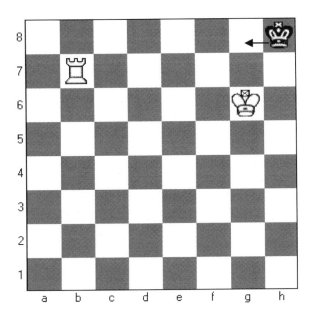

When the enemy king goes to g8, we will have checkmate in 1 move.

Q. Can you see it?

A: Rb8 is checkmate

Endgames

Now let's move on to king and pawn endgames. Before we can win with a queen, we must often promote a pawn first. We are going to look at the key king and pawn endgame positions.

King and Pawn Endgames

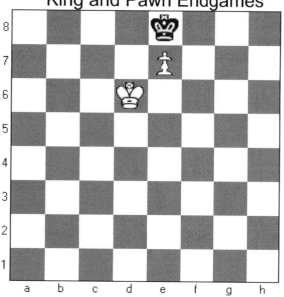

This type of position often happens and you have to remember one thing; each side wants it to be the other sides turn!

If it is Black's move, he will have to move his king away to f7. After that the White king will step up to d7 and he will promote his pawn the following turn.

If it is White's turn, the only square where he can move his king to and still protect his pawn is e6. However, after Ke6, the position is stalemate since Black has no moves.

We are now going to move on to some more complicated key positions to memorize and then a test. Many chess masters find that even they cannot solve all of them correctly and those who do need at least an hour to complete the test. You will have to circle the correct answers in the test. These king and pawn endgames are more complicated than any of the endgames that we have looked at so far. For that reason, all are explained in detail in the answer section.

Good luck!

King and Pawn Endings
Some Key Positions

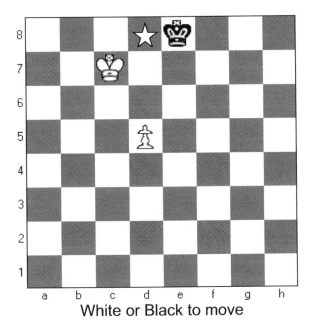

White or Black to move

White controls the queening square (d8)
White Wins

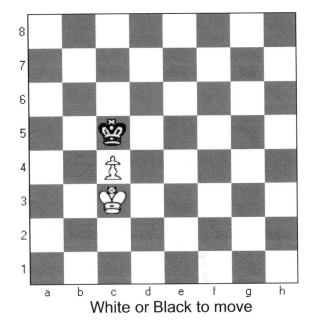

White or Black to move

With the Black king in front of the pawn
it is a **draw** no matter who is to move

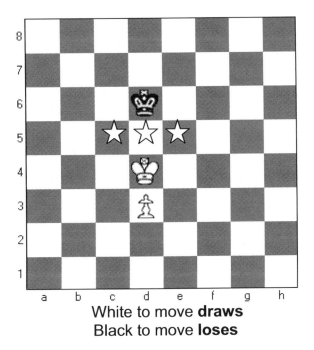

White to move **draws**
Black to move **loses**

The stars represent the key squares of the
pawn. Whoever controls the key squares
determines the outcome.

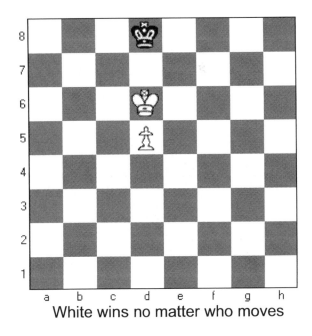

White wins no matter who moves

The king in front of the pawn on the 6th
rank always wins. White will control
the queening square.

King and Pawn Endings-Test

Circle the correct answer below each diagram

#1

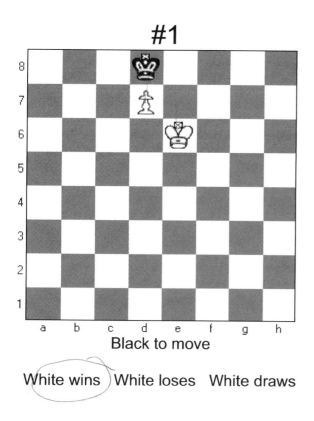

Black to move

(White wins)   White loses   White draws

#2

White to move

White wins   White loses   (White draws)

#3

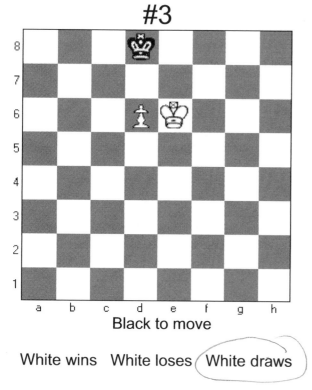

Black to move

White wins   White loses   (White draws)

#4

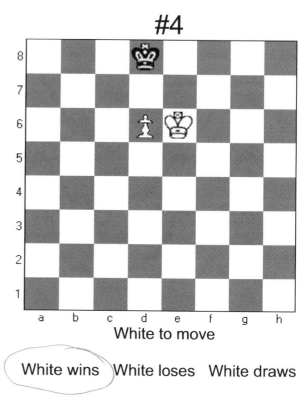

White to move

(White wins)   White loses   White draws

King and Pawn Endings-Test

Circle the correct answer below each diagram

#5

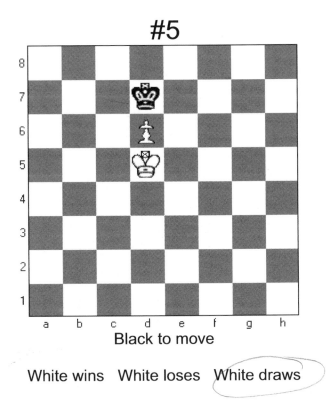

Black to move

White wins   White loses   ~~White draws~~

#6

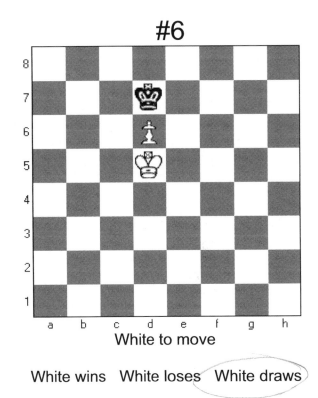

White to move

White wins   White loses   ~~White draws~~

#7

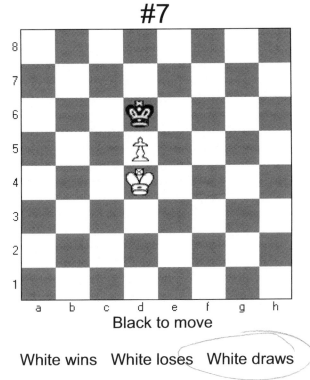

Black to move

White wins   White loses   ~~White draws~~

#8

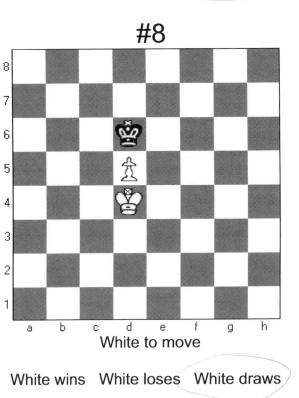

White to move

White wins   White loses   ~~White draws~~

King and Pawn Endings-Test

Circle the correct answer below each diagram

#9

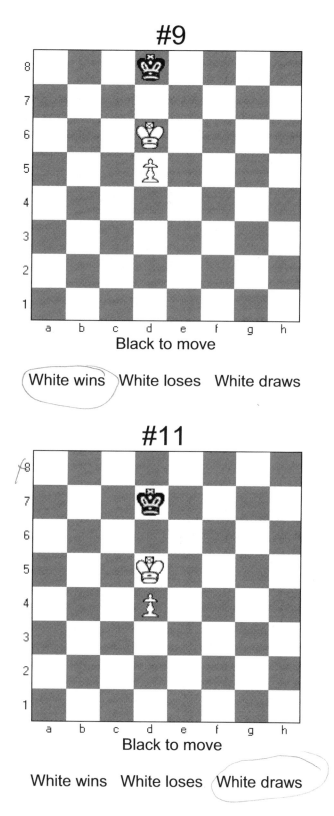

Black to move

(White wins)   White loses   White draws

#10

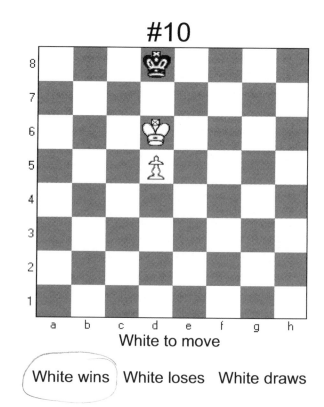

White to move

(White wins)   White loses   White draws

#11

Black to move

White wins   White loses   (White draws)

#12

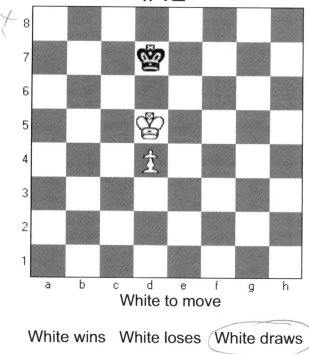

White to move

White wins   White loses   (White draws)

King and Pawn Endings-Test

Circle the correct answer below each diagram

#13

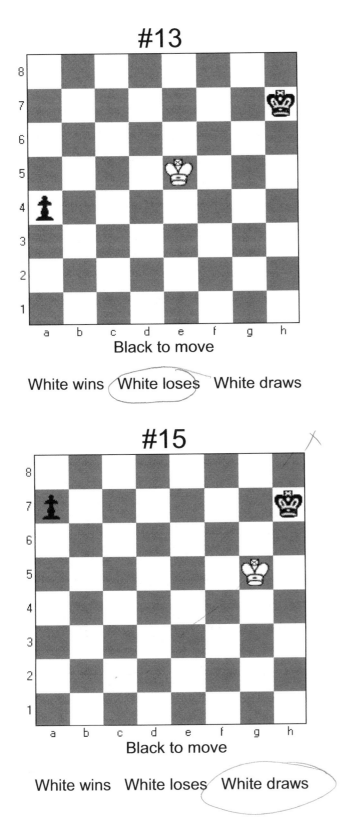

Black to move

White wins   (White loses)   White draws

#14

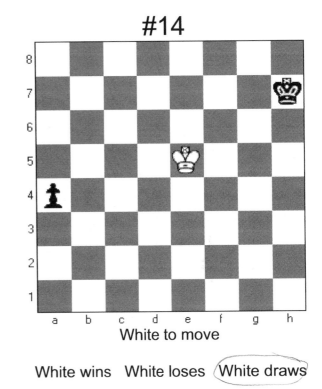

White to move

White wins   White loses   (White draws)

#15

Black to move

White wins   White loses   (White draws)

#16

White to move

White wins   White loses   (White draws)

King and Pawn Endings-Test

Circle the correct answer below each diagram

#17

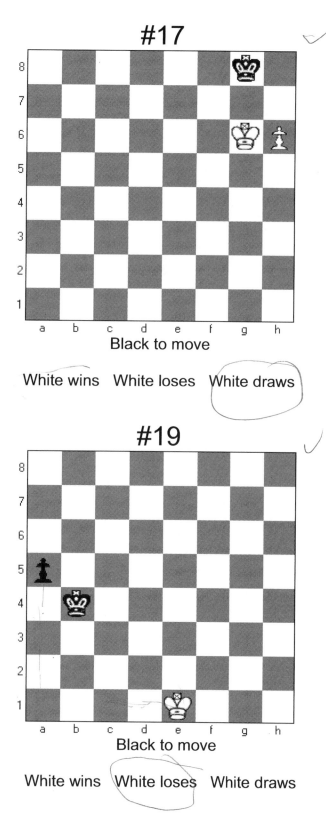

Black to move

White wins   White loses   ~~White draws~~

#18

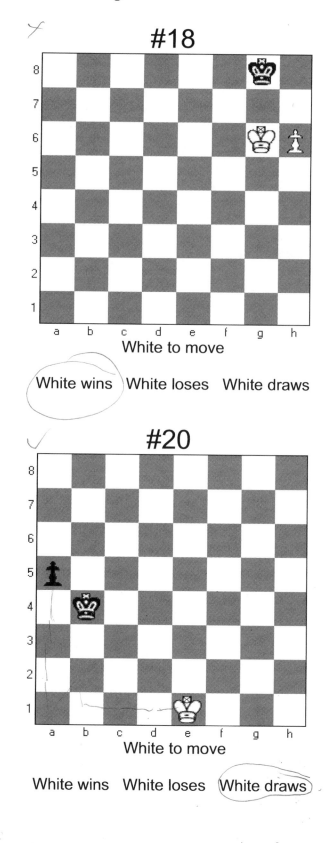

White to move

~~White wins~~   White loses   White draws

#19

Black to move

White wins   ~~White loses~~   White draws

#20

White to move

White wins   White loses   ~~White draws~~

King and Pawn Endings-Test

Circle the correct answer below each diagram

#21

Black to move

White wins   White loses   (White draws)

#22

White to move

White wins   White loses   (White draws)

#23

Black to move

White wins   (White loses)   White draws

#24

White to move

(White wins)   White loses   White draws

King and Pawn Endings-Test

Circle the correct answer below each diagram

#25

Black to move

White wins   White loses   White draws

#26

White to move

White wins   White loses   White draws

#27

Black to move

White wins   White loses   White draws

#28

White to move

White wins   White loses   White draws

King and Pawn Endings-Test

Circle the correct answer below each diagram

#29

Black to move

(White wins) White loses   White draws

#30

White to move

(White wins)   White loses   White draws

#31

Black to move

(White wins)   White loses   White draws

#32

White to move

(White wins)   White loses   White draws

King and Pawn Endings-Test

Circle the correct answer below each diagram

#33

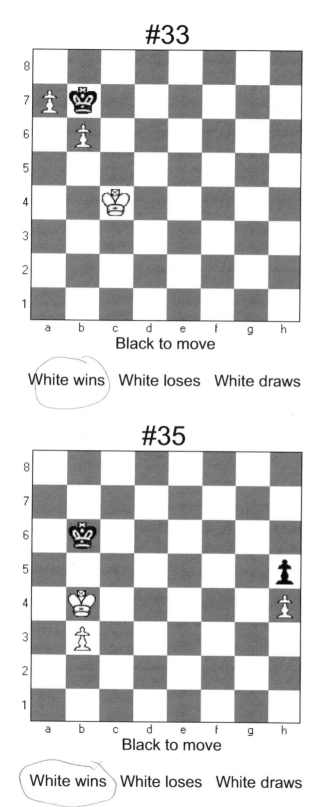

Black to move

White wins   White loses   White draws

#34

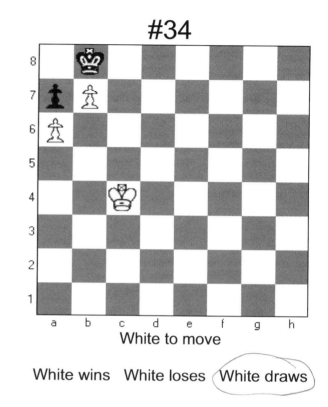

White to move

White wins   White loses   White draws

#35

Black to move

White wins   White loses   White draws

#36

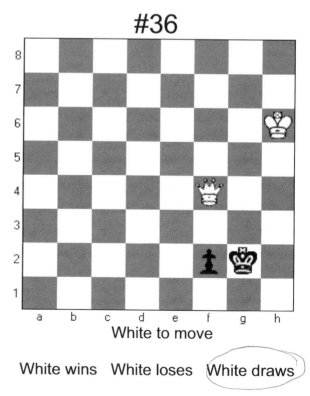

White to move

White wins   White loses   White draws

King and Pawn Endings-Test

Circle the correct answer below each diagram

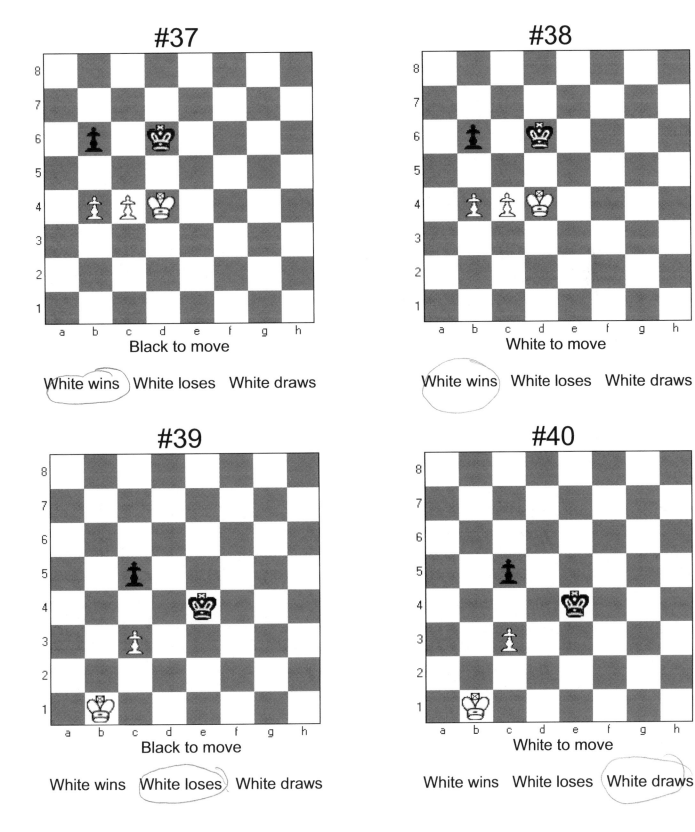

#37

Black to move

(White wins) White loses White draws

#38

White to move

(White wins) White loses White draws

#39

Black to move

White wins (White loses) White draws

#40

White to move

White wins White loses (White draws)

How Much Do You Know About Chess Answers

Page 4
1. A
2. B
3. D
4. C
5. A- castling
6. D
7. A
8. B

Page 5
9. C
10-12. move, block, capture
13. A
14. C
15-16. The ♕ and ♗ can be captured

Page 6
17. The ♗ is attacking the ♚
18. ♚ captures ♖ is Black's only move
19. ♕c8 is the only checkmate
20. ♕xg7 is the only checkmate

Add up your total score. You may start on page 38 if you scored 20 points or more. If you scored less than 20 points, please start at the beginning.

Answers to Exercises

Page 10
#2. ♕c8, ♕d8, ♕e8
#3. ♕xf7, ♕a8, ♖d8
#4. ♕h5, ♘f7, ♔g3

Page 11
#5. ♖xg7, ♗xg7, ♖xf8
#6. ♕g8, ♕xf7, ♙d7
#7. ♕xg7, ♖e8, ♘f6
#8. ♕xf8, ♖xf8, ♕xh7

Page 12
#9. ♔d2, ♔e2, 0-0-0
#10. ♕b7, ♕xa7, ♘a6
#11. ♕b8, ♕h8, ♖h8
#12. ♘h3, ♔d2, 0-0-0

Page 13
#1. ♖d8
#2. ♖f8
#3. ♖f8
#4. ♖h8

Page 14
#5. ♖b8
#6. ♖b-g7
#7. ♖e8
#8. ♖h8

Page 15
#9. ♖xh7
#10. ♖h8
#11. ♖h7
#12. ♖h1

Page 16
#13. ♖d8
#14. ♖d7
#15. ♖d8
#16. ♖xc7

Page 17
#17. ♖h4
#18. ♖c4
#19. ♖h8
#20. ♖a6

Page 18
#21. ♖xc8
#22. ♖d8
#23. ♖e8
#24. 0-0

Page 19
#25. ♕h8
#26. ♕g8
#27. ♕xg7
#28. ♕xg7

Page 20
#29. ♕g7
#30. ♕h8
#31. ♕e6
#32. ♕e6(b3)

Page 21
#33. ♕f8
#34. ♕xa6
#35. ♕e8
#36. ♕g7

Page 22
#37. ♕xh7
#38. ♕g5
#39. ♕h3
#40. ♕d5

Page 23
#41. ♕xh7
#42. ♙e7
#43. ♙xc8=♕   (or ♖)
#44. ♕xb4

Page 24
#45. ♗f6
#46. ♗g6
#47. ♗d4
#48. ♗f6

Page 25
#49. ♗xh7
#50. ♗g5
#51. ♗f6
#52. ♗d7

Page 26
#53. ♗xg5
#54. ♗g6
#55. ♗e5
#56. ♖f8

Page 27
#57. ♘e6
#58. ♙e6
#59. ♗d6
#60. ♗f6

Page 28
#61. ♘f7
#62. ♘f7
#63. ♘h6
#64. ♘d7

Page 29
#65. ♘f7
#66. ♘f7
#67. ♘d6
#68. ♘f6

Page 30
#69. ♘g6
#70. ♘g6
#71. ♘d8
#72. ♘d6

Page 31
#73. ♘g6
#74. ♘f6
#75. ♘f6
#76. ♙xf8=♘

Page 32
#77. ♙g7
#78. ♙f7
#79. ♙g6
#80. ♙xg7

Page 33
#81. ♙f7
#82. ♙gxf7
#83. ♙f7
#84. ♙e4

Page 34
#85. ♕h5
#86. ♕xf7
#87. ♕xf7
#88. ♕xf7

Page 35
#89. ♖h8
#90. ♕h8
#91. ♖d8
#92. ♗b5

Page 36
#93. ♘g6
#94. ♗a5
#95. ♗g6
#96. ♕e8

Page 37
#97. ♕g7
#98. ♕xg6
#99. ♕e5
#100. ♙f8=♘

Page 42
#1. ♙f4
#2. ♙e5
#3. ♙f5

Page 42 cont'd
#4. ♙e5

Page 43
#5. ♙e5
#6. ♙g4
#7. ♙b4
#8. ♙e4

Page 44
#9. ♘g6
#10. ♘f7
#11. ♘f7
#12. ♘c5

Page 45
#13. ♘e7
#14. ♘xd6
#15. ♘e7
#16. ♘e4

Page 46
#17. ♗d5
#18. ♗g5
#19. ♗e4
#20. ♗e5

Page 47
#21. ♗c4
#22. ♗c3
#23. ♗xc6
#24. ♗e5

Page 48
#25. ♖e5
#26. ♖d5
#27. ♖b5
#28. ♖g6

Page 49
#29. ♖e5
#30. ♖d6
#31. ♖xg6
#32. ♖e8

Page 50
#33. ♕e6
#34. ♕d2
#35. ♕d6
#36. ♕xe5

Page 51
#37. ♕e2
#38. ♕c3
#39. ♕d4
#40. ♕xa6

Page 52
#41. ♔e4
#42. ♔h6
#43. ♔f7
#44. ♔d5

Page 53
#45. ♕e2
#46. ♘d5
#47. ♕c5
#48. ♙e6

Page 54
#49. ♕f5
#50. ♕h4
#51. ♕e4
#52. ♕d4

Page 55
#53. 1.♕xd4 ♕xd4
    2.♘xf5
#54. 1.♗b5 ♕xb5
    2.♘d6
#55. 1.♖xg7 ♔xg7
    2.♕d4
#56. 1.♕xh6 ♔xh6
    2.♘f7

Page 56
#57. 1.♗xf6 ♕xf6
    2.♕d5
#58. 1.♖xd6 ♖xd6
    2.♕e5
#59. 1.♕h8 ♔xh8
    2.♘xf7
#60. 1.♕xe7 ♔xe7
    2.♘xd5

Page 57
#61. 1.♕xf6 ♙xf6
    2.♘e7
#62. 1.♖xc6 ♖xc6
    2.♗xd5
#63. 1.♖xh7 ♔xh7
    2.♘xf6
#64. 1.♖c8 ♕xc8
    2.♘xe7

Page 58
#65. 1.♖xc6 ♙xc6
    2.♕xc6
#66. 1.♕e5 ♕xe5
    2.♖xf8
#67. 1.♖xa5 ♔xa5
    2.♘c4

Page 58 cont'd
#68. 1.♗xf7 Kxf7
    (1...♕xf7 2.♘d6)
    2.♘xe5

Page 59
#69. 1.♙e4 ♗xe4
    2.♕a4
#70. 1.♙d6 ♗xd6
    2.♘d5
#71. 1.♕xc6 ♕xc6
    2.♘xe7
#72. 1.♙e4 ♘e7
    2.♙e5

Page 60
#73. 1.♕h8 ♔g5
    2.♕e5
#74. 1.♕xc6 ♙xc6
    2.♘d7
#75. 1.♕xg6 ♔xg6
    2.♘e5
#76. 1.♘xc7 ♔d8
    2.♘e6

Page 61
#77. 1.♖xe8 ♖xe8
    2.♕xe8 ♕xe8
    3.♘f6
#78. 1.♙c4 ♗xc4
    2.♖c1 ♙b5
    3.♙b3
#79. 1.♗xf8 ♔xf8
    2.♗xf7 ♔xf7
    3.♘d6
#80. 1.♖xh4 ♕xh4
    2.♕xf8 ♔xf8
    3.♘g6

Page 62
#81. 1.♗xf6 ♗xf6
    2.♖h7 ♔xh7
    3.♘xf6
#82. 1.♘d5 ♕d8
    2.♖xe6 ♙xe6
    3.♘xe6
#83. 1.♖d8 ♔g7
    2.♖g8 ♔xg8
    3.♘f6
#84. 1.♕c8 ♔g7
    2.♕g8 ♔xg8
    3.♘xf6

194

Page 63

#85. 1.♘f6 ♚f7
    2.♕xg7 ♚xg7
    3.♘e8
#86. 1.♘e7 ♚f7
    2.♕xg7 ♚xg7
    3.♘f5
#87. 1.♖xf6 ♝xf6
    (1...♛xf6 2.♖xd7)
    2.♕g4 any
    3.♖xd7
#88. 1.♖xd5 ♟xd5
    2.♚xd5 ♖c8
    3.♟e6

Page 64

#89. 1.♖xb8 ♖xb8
    2.♝xe7 ♚xe7
    3.♘xc6
    or 1.♖xe7 ♖xe7
    2.♝xe7 ♚xe7
    3.♘xc6
#90. 1.♖f8 ♖xf8
    2.♕xh7 ♚xh7
    3.♟xf8=♘
#91.1.♝f2 ♚d5
    (1...♚e4 2.♘d6)
    2.♝c4 ♚c6
    (2...♚xc4 3.♘d6)
    3.♝b5 ♚xb5
    4.♘d6
#92. 1.♟c4 ♕d4
    (1...♘b(e)xc4
    2.♘c3;
    1...♕xc4 2.♘d2)
    2.♟e3 ♕xc4
    3.♘d2 or 3.♕xe5

Page 68

#1. 1.♖xd8 ♚xd8
    2.♖xh4
#2. 1.♖xe7 ♖e7
    2.♘xd5
#3. 1.♖xg5 ♟xg5
    2.♕xe3
#4. 1.♟d5 ♚xd5
    2.♝xf5

Page 69

#5. 1.♝xc6 ♟xc6
    2.♕xd4
#6. 1.♖xe7 any
    2.♕xd5
#7. 1.♖e8 ♖xe8
    2.♕xd5
#8. 1.♖h8 ♚xh8
    2.♕xf8

Page 70

#9. 1.♘xc5 ♟xc5
    2.♖xd7
#10. 1.♖xc6 ♕(♟)xc6
    2.♘e7
#11. 1.♖xf6 ♕(♟)xf6
    2.♕xh7++
#12. 1.♝xb6 ♟xb6
    2.♝xc4

Page 71

#13. 1.♝xc5 ♕xc5
    2.♖1b7
#14. 1.♘xf6 ♟xf6
    (1...♚h8 2.♘xd5 ♕xc3
    3.♘xc3)
    2.♝xd5 ♝xd5
    3.♕xb4
#15. 1.♕h7 ♚f8
    2.♖xf5 ♟xf5
    3.♕h8 ♚e7
    4.♕xg7 ♚ any
    5.♕xb7
#16. 1.♕xf6 ♘xf6
    2.♟f8=♘ ♚h8
    3.♖g8 ♘g8
    4.♝c3 ♘f6
    5.♝xf6

Page 75

#1. 1.♝c4
#2. 1.♝c4
#3. 1.♟f4
#4. 1.♖e1

Page 76

#5. 1.♕f6++
#6. 1.♝c4
#7. 1.♟f3
#8. 1.♖h8++

Page 77

#9. 1.♖h2 ♚g7(8)
    2.♖ag2
#10. 1.♖d8 ♚h7
    2.♝d3
#11. 1.♖xd5 ♖xd5
    2.♝c4
#12. 1.♕e2 ♟d5
    2.♟d3

Page 78

#13. 1.♝c5 ♝b6
    2.♕f4
#14. 1.♖xh6 ♟xh6
    2.♖g1
#15. 1.♖xf6 ♖xf6
    2.♟g5

Page 78 cont'd

#16. 1.♕b8 ♘xb8
    2.♖d8++

Page 81

#1. 1.♖f1
#2. 1.♖d1
#3. 1.♝b4
#4. 1.♝g2

Page 82

#5. 1.♖xc4 ♟xc4
    2.♕xc4
#6. 1.♖xd4 ♟xd4
    2.♝xd4
#7. 1.♖xe2 ♕xe2
    2.♖e1
#8. 1.♝xe4 ♚xe4
    2.♖e1

Page 84

#2. 1.♖xe8 ♖xe8
    2.♖xe8
#3. 1.♖f8 ♖xf8
    2.♕xf8
#4. 1.♖(♕)xf8 ♖xf8
    2.♕(♖)xf8

Page 85

#5. 1.♖(♕)xf8 ♕xf8
    2.♕(♖)xf8
#6. 1.♖f8 ♖xf8
    2.♖xf8
#7. 1.♖d8 ♝f8
    2.♖d(f)xf8
#8. 1.♖e8 ♝f8
    2.♖xf8

Page 86

#9. 1.♝e6 ♚h8
    2.♖f8
#10. 1.♝e6 ♚h8
    2.♖f8
#11. 1.♝d5 ♚h8
    2.♖f8
#12. 1.♕xf8 ♖xf8
    2.♖c8

Page 87

#13. 1.♕d8 ♝xd8
    2.♖e8
#14. 1.♕b8 ♘xb8
    2.♖d8
#15. 1.♕e8 ♖xe8
    2.♖xe8
#16. 1.♖xh7 ♚xh7
    2.♖h1

Page 88
#17. 1.♖xh7 ♔xh7
2.♖h1
#18. 1.♖xh7 ♔xh7
2.♖h1
#19. 1.♖xh7 ♔xh7
2.♖h1
#20. 1.♕f8 ♖xf8
2.♖xf8

Page 89
#21. 1.♗e6 ♔h8
2.♖xf8
#22. 1.♗e6 ♔h8
2.♖xf8
#23. 1.♗xh7 ♔h8
2.♖xf8
#24. 1.♕xh7 ♔xh7
2.♖h3

Page 90
#25. 1.♕xh7 ♔xh7
2.♖h3
#26. 1.♕xf7 ♖xf7
2.♖e8
#27. 1.♕xf7 ♖xf7
2.♖e8
#28. 1.♕d8 ♔xd8
2.♖f8

Page 91
#29. 1.♕h7 ♔f8
2.♕xf7
#30. 1.♕h7 ♔f8
2.♕xf7
#31. 1.♕xh6 ♔g8
2.♕g7
#32. 1.♕h6 ♔g8
2.♕xg7

Page 92
#33. 1.♖xf8 ♖xf8
2.♖e8
#34. 1.♖h4 ♔g8
2.♖h8
#35. 1.♖xf8 ♔xf8
2.♕d8
#36. 1.♕f8 ♖xf8
2.♖xf8

Page 93
#37. 1.♖h8 ♔xh8
2.♕xf8
#38. 1.♖xh6 ♔xh6
2.♕h8
#39. 1.♕f5 ♙g6
2.♕xf7

Page 93 cont'd
#40. 1.♕xh6 ♙xh6
2.♖h7

Page 94
#41. 1.♕h7 ♔f7
2.♕xg7
#42. 1.♖g8 ♔xg8
2.♕g7 (h8)
#43. 1.♕g8 ♔xg8
2.♖e8
#44. 1.♕xe6 ♙xe6
(1...♗e7 2.♕xe7)
2.♗g6

Page 95
#45. 1.♘xf6 any
2.♕xh7
#46. 1.♘xf6 any
2.♕xh7
#47. 1.♘e7 ♘xe7
2.♖h8
or 1.♖h8 ♘xh8
2.♘e7
#48. 1.♘xf6 any
2.♕xh7

Page 96
#49. 1.♖xe8 ♖xe8
2.♕g7
#50. 1.♖c8 ♕xc8
2.♕xg7
#51. 1.♘e7 ♘xe7
2.♘h6
or 1.♘h6 ♘xh6
2.♘e7
#52. 1.♖c8 ♗xc8
2.♖e8

Page 97
#53. 1.♖xc4 ♕xc4
2.♘xa7
#54. 1.♕xh8 ♘xh8
(1...♘f8 2.♕(♖)xf8)
2.♖f8
#55. 1.♕f6 ♘xf6
(1...♖e7 2.♕xe7)
2.♗e7
#56. 1.♕f5 ♘xf5
(1...♘e6 2.♕xe6)
2.♙e6

Page 98
#57. 1.♕xh7 ♖xh7
(1...♘f8 2.♕f7)
2.♘g6

Page 98 cont'd
#58. 1.♕d8 ♕xd8
(1...♕f8 2.♕xf8)
2.♘g6
#59. 1.♕g2 ♕xg2
(1...♕g4(3) 2.♕xg4(3))
2.♘h6
#60. 1.♕f8 ♗xf8
2.♘xc7

Page 99
#61. 1.♖xf5 ♕xf5
(1...♕g6 2.♕xg6)
2.♖1g7
#62. 1.♗e5 ♖xe5
2.♕f8
or 1.♕f8 ♖xf8
2.♗e5
#63. 1.♖e8 ♘xe8
2.♕xh7
#64. 1.♕xh7 ♕xh7 2.♘f7

Page 100
#65. 1.♖xh7 ♔xh7
2.♕g7
#66. 1.♕f6 ♙xf6
(1...♖e7 2.♕xe7)
2.♘f7
#67. 1.♕f6 ♗xf6
(1...♖g7 2.♕xg7)
2.♘f7
#68. 1.♖f7 ♘xf7
2.♘h7

Page 101
#69. 1.♖h5 ♘xh5
2.♘f5
#70. 1.♖h5 ♗xh5
2.♘f5
#71. 1.♖xg6 ♙xg6
2.♘h6
#72. 1.♕xf8 ♘xf8
2.♘g7

Page 102
#73. 1.♕xh6 ♔g8
2.♕g7
#74. 1.♕xh7 ♔f8
2.♕xg7(h8)
#75. 1.♕f6 ♔g8
2.♖g1
#76. 1.♕xf7 ♔h8
2.♖h1

Page 103
#77. 1.♖f7 ♔g8
2.♕e8

Page 103 cont'd

#78. 1.Rxg8 Kxg8
  2.Qe8
#79. 1.Qxa6 Kb8
  2.Qb7
#80. 1.Qh1 Kg8
  2.Qh7

Page 104

#81. 1.Qxg7 Kxg7
  2.Rg6
#82. 1.Qg7 Rxg7
  2.Rxg7
#83. 1.Ra6 Pxa6
  (1...any B move
  2.Rxa7)
  2.Pb7
#84. 1.Rh5 Pxh5
  2.Qf6

Page 105

#85. 1.Na6 Pxa6
  2.Qb4
#86. 1.Rh8 Nxh8
  2.Qe8
#87. 1.Rh5 Pxh5 (any
   other
  2.Qxh7)
  2.Qf6
#88. 1.Qxg6 Pxg6 (any
   other 2.Qh7)
  2.Rh7

Page 106

#89. 1.Qf8 Nxf8
  2.Ne7
#90. 1.Qf8 Nxf8
  (1...Kh7 2.Qg7)
  2.Ne7
#91. 1.Qxg7 Kxg7
  2.R1f7
#92. 1.Qg6 Pxg5
  (1...any other
  2.Qh7)
  2.Qh5

Page 107

#93. 1.Pb5 Bxb5
  (1...Kxb5 2.Bc4)
  2.Bc8
#94. 1.Rhg7 Ne8
  (1...Nc8 2.Rg8;
  1...Kc8 2.Ra8;
  1...Ke8 2.Rg8)
  2.Ra8
#95. 1.Qa1 any
  2.Qh8
#96. 1.Qc5 Kxc5
  2.Bf8

Page 108

#97. 1.Qh3 Ke4
  2.Rc4
#98. 1.Pc8=N Kc6
  2.Pb5
#99. 1.Qh1 Pd5
  2.Pxd6
#100.1.Qa5 Bc5 (1...Be7(6)
  2.Qe5; 1...Pd6(7)
  2.Qd5;
  1...Bg7(h6)
  2.Qxb41...Be7(d6)
  2.Qxb4; 1...Re6(d7)
  2.Nf5; 1...Pe5
  2.Qxe5; ; 1...Bb7(f5)
  2.Nxf5) 2.Qa1

Page 110

#1. 1.Qxh7 Kxh7
  2.Rh4 Kg8
  3.Rh8
#2. 1.Nc7 Kf8
  2.Qd8 Bd8
  3.Re8
#3. 1.Nxa7 Bxa7
  2.Qxc6 Pxc6
  3.Ba6
#4. 1.Bxh7 Kxh7
  2.Qh5 Kg8
  3.Qh8

Page 111

#5. 1.Rh8 Kxh8
  2.Qh5 Kg8
  3.Qh7
#6. 1.Qxh7 Kxh7
  2.Rh6 Kg8
  3.Rh8
#7. 1.Qxf6 Pxf6
  2.Bh6 Qg7
  3.Rxf6
#8. 1.Qd5 Qxd5
  (1... Pxd5 2.Ra6)
  2.Rd7 Qd6
  3.Pc4

Page 112

#9. 1.Be6 Kc7
  2.Nxc8(c4) Qd6
  3.Qxd6
#10. 1.Rxd5 Pxd5
  2.Nd3 Pxd3
  3.Pf4
#11. 1.Rxf6 Pxf6
  2.B(Q)xh6 Rxh6
  3.Q(B)xh6
#12. 1.Qh4 Rh5
  2.R1f6 Bxf6
  3.Qxf6

Page 113

#13. 1.Nh6 Kh8
  2.Nxf7 Kg8
  3.Rxg7
#14. 1.Qxh7 Kxh7
  2.Bxg5 Kg8(6)
  3.Ne7
#15. 1.Nh5 Rxh5
  2.Rxg6 Kxg6
  3.Re6
#16. 1.Qg5 Qxg5
  2.Re8 Bf8
  3.Rxf8
  (or 1.Re8 Bf8
  {1...Qxe8 2.Qg5}
  2.Qg5 Qxg5
  3.Rxf8

Page 114

#17. 1.Qh8 Ke7
  2.Ng6 Pxg6
  3.Qxg7
#18. 1.Rh8 Bxh8
  (1...Kxh8 2.Qh7)
  2.Qh7 Kf8
  3.Qxh8
#19. 1.Ra7 Kxa7
  2.Re7 Kb8
  3.Qb7
#20. 1.Qh6 Nxh6
  2.Bxh6 Kg8
  3.Pf7

Page 115

#21. 1.Qh6 Rg8
  2.Qxh7 Kxh7
  3.Rh4
#22. 1.Bf6 Pxf6
  2.Kf8 Pf5
  3.Nf7
#23 1.Rg7 any
  2.Rg8 Kxg8
  3.Nf7
#24. 1.Qh6 Bf6
  2.Bxf6 Pxh6
  3.Nxh6

Page 116

#25. 1.Qh5 Qxh5
  2.Ne7 Kh7(8)
  3.Rxh5
#26. 1.Ng5 Pd6
  2.Nxe4 Pxe5
  (2...Nxe4 3.Re8)
  3.Nxf6
#27. 1.Rd7 Nxd7
  2.Nc6 any
  3.Nf6

Page 116 cont'd

#28. 1. ♖h5 ♙xh5
  2. ♗(♕)xf6 ♔xf6
  3. ♕(♗)xf6

Page 117

#29. 1. ♕d8 ♖xd8
  2. ♖xd8 ♖xd8
  3. ♖xd8
#30. 1. ♕xb8 ♖xb8
  2. ♖d8 ♖xd8
  3. ♖xd8
#31. 1. ♕xf8 ♔xf8
  2. ♖d8 ♗xd8
  3. ♖xd8
#32. 1. ♕xg8 ♔xg8
  2. ♖c8 ♕d8
  3. ♖xd8

Page 118

#33. 1. ♕xf8 ♔xf8
  2. ♘d7 ♔g8
  3. ♖e8
#34. 1. ♕xf8 ♔xf8
  2. ♖d8 ♔e7
  3. ♖e8
#35. 1. ♕xg8 ♔xg8
  2. ♗e6 ♔h8
  3. ♖f8
#36. 1. ♖e8 ♗f8
  2. ♗h6 any
  3. ♖xf8

Page 119

#37. 1. ♕d8 ♔xd8
  2. ♖f8 ♗xf8
  3. ♖xf8
#38. 1. ♖b8 ♔e7
  2. ♗c5 ♔f7
  3. ♖f8
#39. 1. ♗xh7 ♘xh7
  (1...♔h8
  2. ♗g8 ♔xg8
  3. ♕h8)
  2. ♕xh7 ♔f8
  3. ♕h8
#40. 1. ♕g5 ♔f7
  2. ♖d7 ♔ any
  3. ♕d8

Page 120

#41. 1. ♘h6 ♔h8
  2. ♕g8 ♖(♘)xg8
  3. ♘f7

Page 120 cont'd

#42. 1. ♘b6 ♔b8
  2. ♕c8 ♖xc8
  3. ♘d7
#43. 1. ♘g3 ♔h2
  2. ♖h1 ♗xh1
  3. ♘f1
#44. 1. ♖b1 ♔a7
  2. ♕d4 ♕xd4
  3. ♘xc6

Page 121

#45. 1. ♖b6 ♘xb6
  2. ♗c3 ♘b4
  3. ♗xb4
#46. 1. ♖h8 ♔xh8
  2. ♕xf8 ♖g8
  3. ♕h6
#47. 1. ♕h7 ♘xh7
  2. ♘g6 ♔g8
  3. ♗d5
#48. 1. ♕xa6 ♙xa6
  2. ♖a7 ♗xa7
  3. ♙b7

Page 122

#49. 1. ♘g5 any ♙xg5
  2. ♖e7 ♔ any
  3. ♕xg7
#50. 1. ♙g7 ♖xg7
  2. ♕h6 ♖h7
  3. ♕xh7
#51. 1. ♘5f6 ♙xf6
  2. ♗xf6 ♔h7
  3. ♕g7
#52. 1. ♕h3 ♔e7
  2. ♘d5 ♔f8
  3. ♕h6

Page 123

#53. 1. ♗c2 ♔e6
  2. ♖xh6 ♙f6
  3. ♘g5
#54. 1. ♘g6 ♔g8
  2. ♘xf6 ♕xf6
  3. ♕f8
#55. 1. ♖e7 ♔f8
  2. ♖e8 ♔xe8
  3. ♕e7
#56. 1. ♕h8 ♔xh8
  2. ♕xh6 ♔g8
  3. ♖d8

Page 124

#57. 1. ♕d8 ♔xd8
  2. ♗g5 ♔e8
  3. ♖d8
#58. 1. ♕d8 ♔xd8
  2. ♗a5 ♔ any
  3. ♖d8
#59. 1. ♕e8 ♔xe8
  2. ♗b5 ♔ any
  3. ♖e8
#60. 1. ♕g7 ♔xg7
  2. ♘f5 ♔g8
  3. ♘h6

Page 125

#61. 1. ♕h6 ♗xh6
  (1...♔g8 2. ♕h8 ♗xh8
  3. ♘h6)
  2. ♘g5 ♔h8
  3. ♖h7
#62. 1. ♘e7 ♔h8
  2. ♘g6 ♙xg6
  3. ♙hxg3
#63. 1. ♕xg7 ♔xg7
  2. ♘f5 ♔g8
  3. ♘h6
#64. 1. ♗b6 ♙xb6
  2. ♘dxf7 ♔e8
  (2...♔c7 3. ♕f6)
  3. ♕d8

Page 126

#65. 1. ♘e7 ♔h8
  2. ♖xh7 ♔xh7
  3. ♖h5
#66. 1. ♕xf8 ♖xf8
  2. ♖xh7 ♔xh7
  3. ♖h1
#67. 1. ♘f7 ♔xf7
  2. ♖xh7 ♔g8
  3. ♖h8
#68. 1. ♕h7 ♔xh7
  2. ♘g6 ♔g8
  3. ♖h8

Page 127

#69. 1. ♕xg8 ♔xg8
  2. ♖h8 ♔xh8
  3. ♗f7
#70. 1. ♕xh6 ♔xh6
  2. ♖h1 ♗h4
  3. ♖xh4
#71. 1. ♖xh7 ♔xh7
  2. ♖h1 ♗h2
  3. ♖xh2
#72. 1. ♕xh7 ♔xh7
  2. ♖h8 ♗h4
  3. ♖xh4

198

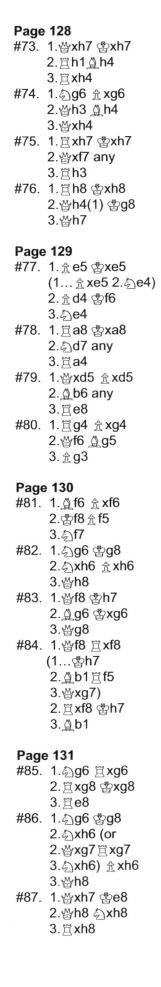

Page 128
#73. 1.♕xh7 ♚xh7
2.♖h1 ♗h4
3.♖xh4
#74. 1.♘g6 ♟xg6
2.♕h3 ♗h4
3.♕xh4
#75. 1.♖xh7 ♚xh7
2.♕xf7 any
3.♖h3
#76. 1.♖h8 ♚xh8
2.♕h4(1) ♚g8
3.♕h7

Page 129
#77. 1.♙e5 ♚xe5
(1… ♟xe5 2.♘e4)
2.♙d4 ♚f6
3.♘e4
#78. 1.♖a8 ♚xa8
2.♘d7 any
3.♖a4
#79. 1.♕xd5 ♟xd5
2.♗b6 any
3.♖e8
#80. 1.♖g4 ♟xg4
2.♕f6 ♗g5
3.♙g3

Page 130
#81. 1.♗f6 ♟xf6
2.♚f8 ♙f5
3.♘f7
#82. 1.♘g6 ♚g8
2.♘xh6 ♟xh6
3.♕h8
#83. 1.♕f8 ♚h7
2.♗g6 ♚xg6
3.♕g8
#84. 1.♕f8 ♖xf8
(1…♚h7
2.♗b1 ♖f5
3.♕xg7)
2.♖xf8 ♚h7
3.♗b1

Page 131
#85. 1.♘g6 ♖xg6
2.♖xg8 ♚xg8
3.♖e8
#86. 1.♘g6 ♚g8
2.♘xh6 (or
2.♕xg7 ♖xg7
3.♘xh6) ♟xh6
3.♕h8
#87. 1.♕xh7 ♚e8
2.♕h8 ♘xh8
3.♖xh8

Page 131 cont'd
#88. 1.♕xg8 ♕xg8
2.♗h4 ♕g5
3.♗xg5

Page 132
#89. 1.♖d1 ♚c6
2.♖db1 any
3.♖1b6
#90. 1.♗xf7 ♚h8
2.♘g6 ♟xg6
3.♖h4
#91. 1.♕f5 ♚e7
(1…♚d6
2.♕xe5 ♚d7
3.♕e6)
2.♕f7
(or 2.♗g5 ♚d6
3.♕xe5
or 2.♕xe5 ♗e6
{2…♚d7 3.♕e6}
3.♕xe6) ♚d6
3.♘e4(b5)
#92. 1.♖h8 ♖f8
2.♗f7 ♚d8
3.♖xf8

Page 133
#93. 1.♖xh6 ♚xh6
(1… ♟xh6 2.♕xf7)
2.♕h8 ♚g5(6)
3.♕h5
#94. 1.♖g6 ♗f6
2.♕xf6 any
3.♕xg7
#95. 1.♚f2 ♟b1=♕
2.♗d5 ♕e4
3.♗xe4
#96. 1.♕xb7 ♘xb7
2.♘c6 ♚a8
3.♘xc7

Page 134
#97. 1.♘f7 ♚g8
2.♘h6 ♚h8
3.♗f6
#98. 1.♘g(e)4 ♟f2
2.♘f6 ♟f1=♕
3.♘g6
#99. 1.♗e6 ♚b8
2.♗d6 ♚a8
3.♗d5
#100. 1.♟xb6 ♚b8
2.♖e8 ♗d8
3.♖xd8

Page 136
#1. 1.♖g1 ♚h4
2.♕g2 ♗d6
3.♕g5 ♚h3
4.♕g3
#2. 1.♘f7 ♚d7
2.♗f5 ♚c6
3.♘d8 ♚d6
4.♗f4
#3. 1.♕e5 ♚xe5
2.♖e7 ♚e6
3.♙f4 ♚e4
4.♖xe6
#4. 1.♘f7 ♚g8
2.♘h6 ♚h8
3.♕g8 ♖xg8
4.♘f7

Page 137
#5. 1.♕b3 ♗d5
2.♙xd6 ♗e6
3.♕xe6 ♚f8
4.♕f7
#6. 1.♕f7 ♚d8
2.♕f8 ♚d7
3.♗e6 ♚xe6
4.♕f7
#7. 1.♖f6 ♘xf6
2.♖xf6 ♚c5
3.♙b4 ♚d4
4.♙c3
#8. 1.♙g3 ♚f3
2.♗e2 ♚g2
3.♖h2 ♚g1
4.♚d(e)2
or 0-0-0

Page 141
#1. 1.♘d5
#2. 1.♗g5
#3. 1.♘d5
#4. 1.♗xg5

Page 142
#5. 1.♗xf7 ♚e7
2.♘d5
#6. 1.♗xf7 ♚e7
2.♗g5
#7. 1.♗xf7 ♚e7
2.♘d5
#8. 1.♗xf7 ♚e7
2.♗xg5

Page 143

#9. 1.♘xe5 ♗xd1
    (1...♙xe5 2.♕xg4)
    2.♗xf7 ♔e7
    3.♘d5++

#10. 1.♘xe5 ♘xe5
    (1...♗xd1
    2.♗xf7♔e7
    3.♘d5++;
    1...♙xe5
    2.♕xh5)
    2.♕xh5 ♘xc4
    3.♕b5 followed by
    ♕xc4 and White
    is up a ♙

#11. 1.♘xe5 ♗xd1
    (1...♙xe5
    2.♕xg4)
    2.♗xf7 ♔e7
    3.♘d5++

#12. 1.♘xe5 ♗xd1
    (1...♙xe5
    2.♕xg4)
    2.♗xf7 ♔e7
    3.♗g5++

Page 145

#1. Kf1 [K] h1 (K) d1
  ♕d2++

#2. Kf1 [K] a2 (K) h3
  ♖h1++

#3. Kd3 [K] a1 (K) h8
  ♕f8++

#4. Kh8 [K] f8 (K) f8
  ♙g7++ or (K) h6
  ♙f8=♕(♗)++

Page 146

#5. Ke8 [K] a7 (K) d4
  ♕c3++

Page 146 cont'd

#6. Kh8 [K] f8 (K) c8
  ♖h8++

#7. Kf6 [K] d6 (K) a1
  ♖e2++

#8. Kh6 [K] h8 (K) f8
  ♙h8=♕(♖)++

Page 148

#1. 1.♘f7 ♔g8
   2.♘h6 ♔h8
   3.♕g8 ♖xg8
   4.♘f7

Page 149

#2. 1.♙g3 ♔f3
   2.♗e2 ♔g2
   3.♖h2 ♔g1
   4.♔d(e)2 or 0-0-0

Page 150

#3. 1.♖h8 ♔xh8
   2.♕h2 ♕h6
   3.♕xh6 ♔g8
   4.♕h7

Page 151

#4. 1.♘g6 ♔g8
   (1...♙xg6
   2.♖xh7♔xh7
   3.♖h1)
   2.♘e7 ♔h8
   3.♖xh7 ♔xh7
   4.♖h1

Page 152

#5. 1.♗c4 ♙xc4
   (1...♔h8
   2.♖f8 ♖xf8
   3.♖xf8)
   2.♕xc4 ♔h8
   3.♖f8 ♖xf8
   4.♖xf8

Page 153

#6. 1...♖xg2
   2.♔xg2 (2.♔h1 ♖xh2
   3.♔g1 ♕f2) ♕f2
   3.♔h1 ♕f1
   4.♖xf1

Page 154

#7. 1.♖c8 ♔h7
   2.♖h8 ♔xh8
   3.♕h6 ♔g8
   4.♕xg7

Page 155

#8. 1.♗e7 ♔e8
   2.♗f6 ♔f8
   3.♕e7 ♔g8
   4.♕xg7

Page 156

#9. 1.♕xf8 ♔xf8
   (1...♗xf8 2.♗xf7)
   2.♖xf7 ♔g8
   3.♖g7 ♔ any
   4.♖g8

Page 157

#10. 1...♗e4
   2.♔f1 ♗f5
   3.♕e2 ♗h3
   4.♔e1 ♖g1

#1. White Wins. Black's ♚ must leave the blockading square ex.) 1...♚c7 2.♚e7 with ♙d8=♛ to follow.

#2. White Draws. ♚d6 is the only way to save the ♙, but then it is stalemate.

#3. White Draws. 1...♚e8 keeping the **opposition** (the ♚'s are opposite) 2.♙d7 ♚d8 and we see the same position as from problem #2.

#4. White Wins. 1.♙d7 and we have the same position as from problem #1.

#5. White Draws- 1...♚d8 2.♚e6 (2.♚c6 ♚c8) ♚e8 3.♙d7 ♚d8 which leads us to problem #2 when with White to move it is a draw. Notice that keeping the opposition is important.

#6. White Draws- Whether White plays ♚e5 or ♚c5 the Black ♚ will go back to d8 and we will get the same situation as in problem #5. It is important to remember to go straight back from the ♙.

#7. White Draws-The same position from problems # 5 and #6 will be reached. Black just needs to remember to move straight back from the ♙.

#8. White Draws- It makes no difference who is to move. Black's ♚ will still move straight back from the ♙ and we will reach the same position as in problems #5 and #6.

#9. White Wins- 1...♚c8 (1...♚e8 2.♚c7 and then the ♙ will push to promote) 2.♚e7 and the ♙ will push to promote. Whichever way the Black ♚ moves, the White ♚ will zigzag the other way.

#10. White Wins- 1.♚e6 ♚e8 2.♙d6 ♚d8 3.♙d7 and we have the same position as from problem #1 when Black must leave the queening square. Notice that if the White ♚ is in front of the ♙ on the 6th rank, then White wins no matter who is on move.

#11. White Wins- 1...♚c7 (1...♚e7 2.♚c6) 2.♚e6 and we see the same zigzag technique mentioned in problem #9.

#12. White Draws- 1.♚e5 ♚e7 (the opposition) 2.♙d5 ♚d7 3.♙d6 ♚d8 (straight back from the ♙) and this should look familiar!

#13. White Loses- 1...♙a3 2.♚d4 ♙a2 3.♚c3 ♙a1=♛ White was too slow in catching the ♙ before it promoted. Without counting the moves, you could have figured this problem if you know the 'inside the square' rule. The Black ♙ is on a4 so we can draw a line from a4 to d4, then d4 to d1, then d1 to a1 and finally a1 to a4. There are 4 squares up the board and four to the side. We can see that the White ♚ is not inside the square and therefore cannot catch the ♙.

#14. White Draws- With White to move he can play 1.♚d4 and now he is inside the square. You can count out the moves to see that when Black promotes the ♙, it will be captured by the White ♚.

#15. White Loses- With Black to move he can play 1...♙a5 and after 2.♚f4 the White ♚ is not inside the square.

#16. White Draws- 1.♚f4 ♙a5 2.♚e3 and White is inside the square.

#17. White Draws- 1...♚h8 2.♙h7 stalemate. Since there is no 'I' file for the Black ♚ to move to, the position is drawn.

#18. White Draws-1.♙h7 ♚h8 2.♚h6 stalemate. If the ♙ is a rook ♙ (the a or h ♙), the position is drawn no matter who is to move is the defending ♚ blocks the queening square.

#19. White Loses- 1...♚b3 (1...♙a4 2.♚d1 ♙a3 3.♚c1 and we see that the White ♚ is inside the square and will capture the Black ♙ when it promotes) 2.♚d1 ♚b2 and then the ♙ will run in to promote. The Black ♚ keeps the White ♚ from getting to the ♙. This is called **shouldering**.

#20. White Draws- 1.♚d1 ♚b3 2.♚c1 (threatening ♚b1 when we already know it is a draw) ♚a2 (trying to shoulder the White ♚) 3.♚c2 ♙a4 4.♚c1 ♙a3 5.♚c2 ♚a1 6.♚c1 ♙a2 7.♚c2 and White stalemates Black!

#21. White Loses- 1...♚e5 (1...♚e6 2.♚g7 and Black's ♚ will have to leave the defense of his ♙) 2.♚g7 (the only way to defend his ♙) ♚e6 and White's ♚ must leave the defense of his ♙. Once Black's ♚ captures White's ♙, he will be able to promote his own ♙. Notice how in the position with the ♚'s on e6 and g7, each player wants it to be the other players move. This is called **zugzwang**.

#22. White Wins- 1.♚g8 ♚e6 2.♚g7 and it is Black who is in zugzwang now!

#23. White Draws- 1...♔e2 (it seems hard to understand that the ♔ will move away from where the ♙'s are, but if 1...♔g2 then 2.♔g4 and White will capture Black's ♙ then move out of the way and advance and promote his own ♙) 2.♔g4 ♔e3 3.♔xh4 ♔f4 and we will see the same type of stalemate as in problem #20.

#24. White Draws- 1.♔g4 ♔e3 and we have the same position as in problem #23.

#25. White Draws- 1...♔f8 (1...♔e7 2.♔e5 ♔f7 3.♔f5 ♔e7 4.♔g6 the zigzag again!) 2.♔f5 (2.♔e5 ♔e7) ♔f7 and Black has the opposition. This is the same type of problem as in #12.

#26. White Draws- 1.♔e5 (1.♔f5 ♔f7) ♔e7 and Black has the opposition again and draws just as in the last problem.

#27. White Wins- 1...♔f8 2.♔f5 ♔f7 3.♙f4 (White has a turn to waste!) ♔e7 4.♔g6 and again we have a zigzag that will allow us to get our ♔ in front of the ♙ on the 6th rank.

#28. White Wins- 1.♔f5 ♔f7 2.♙f4 and Black is in zugzwang just as in the last problem.

#29. White Wins- 1...♔c8 2.♔c6 ♔d8 3.♙d7 and we have the same type of position as in problem #1.

#30. White Wins- 1.♙d7 ♔a8 2.♙d8=♕ or ♖ ++

#31. White Wins- 1...♔b8 2.♔b6 ♔a8 (the trickiest move since 2...♔c8 3.♙c7 just leads to our basic losing position) 3.♔c7 (3.♙c7 would be stalemate!) ♔a7 4.♔d7 and the ♙ will just advance to promote

#32. White Wins- 1.♔b5 (1.♔b6 ♔b8 is a draw) ♔a7 (1...♔b8 2.♔b6 would lead us to problem #31) 3.♔c5 ♔b8 4.♔d6 ♔c8 5.♙c7. This one was tricky!

#33. White Wins- 1.♔c5 ♔a8 2.♔b5 (2.♔c6 is stalemate) ♔b7 3.♙a8=♕ ♔xa8 4.♔c6 ♔b8 5.♙b7. Notice how White can only win by sacrificing a ♙. The White ♔ cannot get close otherwise due to stalemate.

#34. White Draws- 1.♔c5 ♔c7 2.♔d5 ♔b8 3.♔e6 ♔c7 and the White ♔ cannot get close without stalemate. Here, sacrificing the ♙ with ♙b8=♕ does not help.

#35. White Wins- 1...♔c6 2.♔c4 ♔b6 3.♔d4 ♔b5 4.♔e4 ♔b4 5.♔f4 ♔xb3 6.♔g5 ♔c4 7.♔xh5 ♔d5 8.♔g6 ♔e6 9.♙h5 ♔e7 10.♙h6 (or simply 10.♔g7 shouldering the Black ♔) ♔f8 11.♙h7 and White's ♙ will promote. Notice that the ♙ that wins for White is not his passed ♙. That ♙ is used as a decoy. By the time the Black ♔ captures White's passed ♙, White already has one on the other side.

#36. White Draws- 1.♕g4 ♔h1 2.♕f3 ♔g1 2.♕g3 ♔h1 and if 3.♕xf2 then it's a stalemate. This is only due to the fact that Black's ♙ has made it to the 7th rank and that it's a Bishop ♙. A Rook ♙ will also due to draw. This is because of the stalemate trick mentioned from this problem. If we shifted all of the pieces over by one row to the left then White would win. Ex) 1.♕f4 ♔g1 2.♔e3 ♔f1 3.♕f3 ♔e1 (now if 3...♔g1 then simply 4.♕xe2 and no stalemate) 4.♔f5 and each time the Black ♔ blocks his ♙ from promoting, the White ♔ will get so move a step closer. Try playing this out on your board at home.

#37. White Wins- 1...♔c6 2.♔e5 ♔c7 (2...♙b5 3.♙c5) 3.♔d5 ♔d7 (Black has the opposition but White has a move to waste) 4.♙b5 ♔c7 5.♔e6 ♔b7 6.♔d6 ♔b8 7.♔c6 ♔a7 8.♔c7 ♔a8 9.♔xb6.

#38. White Wins- 1.♙b5 ♔e6 (1...♔c7 2.♔e5 ♔d7 3.♔d5 ♔c7 4.♔e6 and we see the same idea as in problem #37. 1...♔e7 2.♔e5 ♔d7 is the same) 2.♙c5 ♙xc5 3.♔xc5 ♔d7 4.♔b6 then ♔a7 and the ♙ promotes or even 4.♙b6 ♔c8 5.♔c6 ♔b8 6.♙a7 and we know what happens next.

#39. White Loses- 1...♙c4 (1...♔d3 2.♙c4 ♔xc4 3.♔c2 and White as the opposition- Black must be able to capture the ♙ on the 6th rank) 2.♔c2 ♔e3 and Black's ♔ will push White's ♔ out of the way as in the last problem.

#40. White Draws- 1.♙c4 (the only move that draws; 1.♔b2 ♙c4 2.♔a3 ♔e3 3.♔a4 ♔d2 4.♔b4 ♔d3 and White is in zugzwang.

How the Pieces Move

 **King**
(The game)

(One space at a time)

 **Queen**
(9 points)

 **Rook**
(5 points)

 **Bishop**
(3 points)

 **Knight**
(3 points)   (Moves like the letter 'L'-The knight can also jump)

 **Pawn**

Move
1 space forward, or two on its first turn

Capture (1 point)
One space only

Glossary

Absolute Pin: The pinned piece cannot legally move because it is pinned to the king.

Algebraic: A type of chess notation which uses a grid with coordinates, employing letters and numbers, to describe squares on a chessboard. This workbook is written using algebraic notation.

Back Rank: The last rank on the chessboard (White's back rank is the 1st rank and Black's is the 8th rank).

Bishop: A piece that moves diagonally on one color only. Each player has two bishops at the start of the game.

Blockading Square: A square that stops a pawn from pushing.

Board: What chess is played on; it is divided into 64 squares; a White square should always be in the right hand corner. Remember 'White is on the right'.

Capture: To take an opponent's piece off the board and out of play.

Castle: A special move in which a king and a rook move at the same time.

Check: Attacking the king.

Checkmate: Attacking the king when the king has no way out of danger.

Chess Notation: See notation.

Develop: To move the chess pieces into the game.

Deflection: Getting an opponent's piece to move from an advantageous square.

Double attack: Using one piece to attack two enemy pieces at one time.

Double check: Checking the king with two different pieces at the same time. A triple check cannot occur in a legal position.

En passant: The 'invisible' capture. When a pawn moves two spaces next to an enemy pawn, that enemy pawn can capture it as if it had moved only one space.

Endgame: The part of the game when most of the pieces have been taken off the board. If a game has not already ended, it will end in the endgame.

File: The vertical columns which are labeled A to H on the chessboard.

Fischer: The first American world chess champion.

Fork: Using one piece to attack two or more enemy pieces at one time.

Glossary

Grandmaster: The highest level title that can be achieved in chess. Typically, Grandmasters have chess ratings of about 2600.

Happy Birthday: A big mistake by one's opponent.

Heavy pieces: Another term for the rooks and queens.

International Master: Someone who has received the title of master throughout the world and the 2nd highest level that can be achieved in chess. Typically International Masters have chess ratings of about 2500.

King: The most important piece in a chess game.

Knight: The only piece that can jump over pieces in a chess game.

Legall's mate: A specific pattern that arises when one side sacrifices the queen to checkmate with one bishop and 2 knights. It is name after Legall who was a French chess player during the 1700's.

Master: Someone who has mastered the game of chess. A chess master's rating must be at least 2200 in the United States.

Middlegame: The part of the game that occurs after the opening and before the endgame.

Minor pieces: Another term for the knights and bishops.

Morphy: Considered by many to be the first unofficial world champion. He beat all the best players in the world during the mid 1800's.

Notation: The method used to record a game. See algebraic.

Opening: The beginning part of a chess game. The opening usually ends once a player has developed his minor pieces and castled.

Opposition: When two kings are opposing each other and each player wants the other to move.

Pawn: The weakest piece on a chessboard.

Philidor: A famous player, who lived in France during the 1700's. A student of Legall.

Pin: A chess tactic where a player threatens an opponent's piece, and if that endangered piece moves, a more valuable piece or threat is exposed.

Pawn promotion: An event that occurs when a pawn reaches the opponents first rank. A pawn can then promote itself to a queen, rook, bishop, or knight.

Glossary

Remove the guard: Capturing an enemy piece that is stopping (guarding) an opponent from getting a checkmate or another important threat.

Queen: The most powerful chess piece.

Queen and Helper Checkmate: A type of checkmate where the queen is helped by another one of her pieces.

Rank: The horizontal columns which are labeled 1 to 8 on the chessboard.

Rating: A number given in chess based on results in chess tournaments. Ratings range from 100 to 2850 (the World Champion). 1000 is a respectable rating for a scholastic player. 2200 or higher is the rating of a chess master.

Rook: A piece that moves along ranks and files only.

Scholastic: Any chess player up to the age of 18.

Shouldering: Keeping a king away from a valuable square or piece with one's own king.

Skewer: The opposite of a pin. In this chess tactic, the more valuable piece is in front of the less valuable piece when under attack.

Smothered Checkmate: A type of checkmate where a king is smothered in by his own pieces and checkmate is usually delivered by a knight since a knight cannot be blocked from checking.

Square clearance: Removing one's own piece from a square in order that that square be used for a different piece that can deliver checkmate.

Stalemate: The end of a game when one player is on move but has no legal moves. The result of the game is a tie.

Tactics: A type of trick in chess. Pins and Skewers are examples of chess tactics.

Tournament: Many players compete and a player will play against more than one opponent.

Tournament player: Someone who competes in chess tournaments. A tournament player will have a chess rating.

Trap: A series of moves that leads to a favorable outcome for the person who sets it.

Variation: A line of play in a chess game. Sometimes a player will need to see many variations.

Zugzwang: German for "compulsion to move." A player is in zugzwang if any move will lead to a loss.

Made in the USA
Lexington, KY
04 June 2013